May 13, 1995.

Dearest Karen,

Happy 35th
Birthday!

with love, and
wishes that you will
someday visit the
magical land of
Ireland,

Cathy
xxx

# IRELAND
An Encyclopedia for the Bewildered

# IRELAND

An Encyclopedia
for the Bewildered

## K. S. DALY

AURUM PRESS

*I dtír na ndall is rí fear na leathshúile.*

In the land of the blind, the one-eyed man is king.

– Irish proverb

## ABATTOIR
The inviting first entry in the Golden Pages Classified Telephone Directory for the Dublin area. The final entry is, ironically, the Royal Zoological Society of Ireland.

## ABBEY THEATRE
The Irish National Theatre is famous the world over. Founded by **Lady Gregory** and **W.B. Yeats** in 1904, it was the first English-speaking repertory theatre in the world. Having seen its share of drama, including full-scale riots, the Abbey burnt down in 1951, but was rebuilt and reopened to the public in 1966. The original theatre was built on the site of a morgue.

(See **Peter Pan**)

## ACHILL ISLAND
At just over 56 square miles, Achill is the largest island off the Irish coast. Celebrated for its isolated beauty, it has been home over the years to many writers and artists, among them Germany's Nobel Prize for Literature recipient Heinrich Böll (1917–85), whose *Irisches Tagebuch*, or *Irish Diary*, continues to be an

enormous bestseller in Germany, and Irish painter Paul Henry whose scenes of the island are deservedly famous.

(See **Boycott**; **Sprat**)

## ACTING

The Gate Theatre in Dublin was founded in 1928 by actor/director Hilton Edwards (1903–82) and actor/playwright Micheal MacLiammóir (1899–1978), collectively known as 'The Boys'. Arguably the two most influential figures in Irish theatre this century, Edwards and MacLiammóir were also perhaps the two most colourful. MacLiammóir, who distinguished himself as much by his eccentricity as by his acting, had the habit of wearing yellowish make-up, variously coloured kimonos and a toupee from which he would not be parted (so to speak). On one occasion, late in his career, having secured the role of a bald man in the television serial *Tolka Row*, he refused to remove the toupee and instead insisted on wearing a bald headpiece over it. However, the gay couple's behaviour, rather than causing scandal in Catholic Ireland, earned them a place of respect, and the enormous world success of MacLiammóir's one-man show, *The Importance of Being Oscar*, in 1960, proved, if proof were needed, that this respect had been justified. It was not until after his death, however, that it was discovered the greatest role in MacLiammóir's life had been his life itself, for Micheal MacLiammóir was, in fact, Alfred Willmore who had been born not in Cork, but in Kensal Green, London, and had come as a young man to Ireland where he had simply invented his past. He chose the given name Micheal – the Irish form of Michael – after playing the role of Michael in **Peter Pan** and, it is said, chose Cork as his birthplace because his mother's maiden name was Lee, the river on which that city is built. The rest of his life was spent acting.

There was much acting in Edwards's life also. Born in Holloway Road, North London, Edwards, who was in fact christened Robert (though Hilton was his second name), invented or exaggerated many aspects of his life, from education to military history. But the deceptions may not have begun with him. On his birth certificate his mother describes his father as a Christmas card designer though, in fact, he was Joint Magistrate (Second Grade) in Calcutta. The Boys, acting aside, were, in 1973, the first artists to be made Freemen of the City of Dublin.

## AE

(See **Russell, George**)

## AIRCRAFT

The history of Irish airplane flight is ironically linked to the County of Down. The first airplane flight in Ireland took place at Hillsborough in that county in 1909, covering a distance of 100 yards at just 10 feet off the ground. However, the beginning of Irish aviation history must have been quite shaky because it wasn't long before Sir James Martin from Crosscar, again in Co. Down, felt the need to invent the ejector seat.

Possibly because helicopters do not require runways to take off and land, and are therefore less likely to provide a shaky ride, one Mary Sweeney from Hollywood, again in Co. Down, took her first flight in one belonging to the British army in May 1978. She was 103 years of age.

A man who presumably also enjoyed his flight in a helicopter was Joe Twomey. Twomey, who was IRA chief of staff, made his escape in one in 1973 over the walls of Dublin's Mountjoy Prison.

(See **Fairy Forts**)

## AMAZING GRACE
Popular hymn.

A Co. Clare priest, Fr James Grace was, in 1992, appointed chaplain to the English-speaking community at EuroDisney, just outside of Paris. Walt Disney himself, the founder of the Disney empire, had an Irish-American mother, Mary Richardson, who gave birth to him on 5 December 1905.

## AMERICA
Whatever about the possibility that **St Brendan** 'the Navigator' was the first European to reach America some nine hundred years before Columbus, four of the signatories of the American Declaration of Independence, George Taylor, Matthew Thornton, Charles Thompson and James Smith, did come from Ireland. For that matter, the man who printed the broadsheets for the Declaration was John Dunlap from Strabane. And America's first daily newspaper, *The Pennsylvania Packet*, also came off his presses.

Another Irishman, John Barry (1745–1803) from Wexford, in 1782 superintended the founding of the US Navy.

The Irish factor in the 'greening of America' can easily be seen when one considers that a total of 155 counties in the United States are called after Irish surnames, and there are at least 17 Dublins scattered across the country, in one of which, in North Carolina, alcohol is banned.

## AMERICAN PRESIDENTS
A third of American Presidents have been of Irish descent – Ronald Reagan being the most recent – and the only American President not born on American soil was one of them. His name was Andrew Jackson. Jackson's father, also Andrew Jackson, came to America from Carrickfergus in 1765, and it was claimed that his son was born in the new country.

However, there is some speculation that Jackson may actually have been born on the ship *en route* to the New World, and that he later lied about the date in order to stand for President. Only someone born on American soil is permitted to hold the supreme office.

Another man who held the office was David Riche Atchison, who again had Irish blood. Atchison was President of the United States of America on 4 March 1849. For one day. The following morning he was just David Riche Atchison again. Zachary Taylor, who had been due to succeed President Polk, decided he did not want to start his term with the weekend approaching, so Atchison was sworn in temporarily, making him the shortest-lived President in the country's history.

**AMPUTATION**
Sir Arthur Aston, the commander of Drogheda in its resistance to Cromwell, was beaten to death with his own wooden leg when Cromwell's troops sacked the town in 1649.

Michael Davitt (1846–1906), the land agitator, lost his arm in a machine accident in a cotton mill at the age of eleven.

The head of St Oliver Plunkett (1629–81) survives and is on show in a gold and glass casket in Drogheda Cathedral, while his vestments are preserved in Mullingar Ecclesiastical Museum. Plunkett was hanged, drawn and quartered for his supposed part in the Irish Popish Plot.

The amputated leg of a dead cow or calf was often hung in a cowhouse to protect the surviving stock against evil.

## ANKLES
There has been much comment on the subject of ankles, particularly those of Irish women. *Brewer's Dictionary of Phrase and Fable*, 3rd edition, which explains Irish Legs as 'thick and clumsy ones', quotes Grose on the matter: 'Irish women have a dispensation from the pope to wear the thick end of their legs downwards.'

Earlier still than this observation, one Richard Twiss in his *Tour in Ireland* (1776) says: 'As to the natural history of the Irish species, they are only remarkable for the thickness of their legs, especially those of plebeian females.'

In our own time the American poet John Berryman (1914–72), who lived for a time in Dublin, has been perhaps the most direct of all: 'The Irish have the thickest ankles in the world' ('Dream Song 299').

## APHRODISIAC
The ground **liver** of a black cat, imbibed in a solution, is traditionally said to be a powerful aphrodisiac.

## ARD FHÉIS
High or national assembly. Usually the Annual General Meeting of a political party. The word *féis* originally meant 'fuck'.

## ART
The art collector Hugh Lane, a nephew of **Lady Gregory**, left a collection of paintings to Dublin Corporation on condition that they be housed in a gallery to be built spanning the River Liffey. When the Corporation refused the terms the collection went to the National Gallery in London instead, but, since an agreement in 1959, it moves between there and Dublin's Hugh Lane Municipal Gallery which is named for him. Lane was born on 9 November, or Sadie Hawkins Day. In the United States this is the

day when girls ask boys to dance. A popular slogan during the dance music revival of the early 1980s was 'F*** art, let's dance'.

## ASGILL, JOHN (1658–1738)

An English-born barrister who read with great attention chapter 11 of the Gospel of St John, verses 25–26: 'I am the resurrection and the life; he that believeth in me, though he were dead, yet shall he live: and whosoever liveth and believeth in me shall never die.' Asgill took this in the light of English law to be a valid and binding contract between God and himself and was convinced that, because he *did* believe in God, therefore he would not die. Armed with this certainty he put his thoughts together in a book with the extraordinarily long title *An Argument proving that according to the Covenant of Eternal Life revealed in the Scriptures, man may be translated into the Eternal Life without passing through Death.* On his arrival in Ireland in 1700, largely to avoid the unfavourable reactions of his fellow Englishmen to the book, Asgill was horrified to find the Irish House of Commons passing a resolution to ban it and ordering its immediate destruction by fire at the hand of the hangman. Wisely, Asgill dropped his enquiries and went into politics.

## ATHLONE

Godert de Ginkel (1630–1703) who accompanied William of Orange to Ireland in 1689 and who took the town of Athlone in June 1691 had, until recently, a disco named after him there. The town itself, it is said, gets its name from an episode in the Irish epic, the *Táin*, in which the remains of a much sought-after bull are spread across the length and breadth of Ireland. A section of the carcass arrived in this Shannon-straddling town which thereafter carried the name which some translate as the 'Ford of the Loins'.

**ATLANTIC**
The pilot of the first-ever plane to make an east–west crossing of the Atlantic in 1928 was a Dubliner, James Fitzmaurice.

**AUK, GREAT**
There are rival claims for the sighting of the last Great Auk. Most say that the last was killed off the coast of Iceland on 4 June 1844, but others say a Great Auk was killed on the Saltee Islands off the coast of Wexford by fishermen in 1845. What is sure is that the bird, which had once been a common enough sight off the shores of Ireland, had completely vanished by 1850.

**AUSTRALIA**
There seem to be strong connections between Australia and the Irish county of Laois, since two of its sons, Peter Lalor (b. 1823) and David Collins (b. 1756) have been honoured on postage stamps there. However, in the 8th century, the mere suggestion that people might live 'under the earth' was enough to have the Irish monk Fergal threatened with expulsion from the church.

(See **Prime Ministers; Sinn Féin**)

## BACHELORS

The enormously popular Dublin trio, The Bachelors, had a No.1 hit single with 'Diane' in February 1964, and seven other top ten hits in a three-year period in the early 1960s. They were all in fact married men.

(See **Paisley, Rev. Ian**)

## BACON AND CABBAGE

Francis Bacon (1909–92), the Irish-born painter, was well known for his paintings of meat and his cadaver-like portraits, but it is not believed that he ever painted this traditional Irish meal.

## BÁINÍN

Aran jersey. An item of knitwear worn traditionally by west of Ireland fishermen. The jersey features a traditional pattern unique to each of the families and intended to help identify their bodies if drowned. Now worn almost exclusively by German hippies, UCD science students and on RTE soap operas.

## BALDNESS

(See **Acting**; **Urine**; **Eriugena, Johannes Scotus**)

## BALLINSPITTLE

Co. Cork town which was the site of the first of a spate of moving statues following a sighting by two women out for an evening stroll on 23 June 1985. While the Catholic Church did not officially endorse the sightings, its members (i.e. the Catholic church with a small 'c') did transform the sites into places of pilgrimage for thousands. The rash of sightings eventually healed but left a peculiar scar on the Irish religious mind. A confection seen to be on sale from the back of one van in Ballinspittle during the period of the above-mentioned sightings was dubbed the 'Grotto Burger'.

## BALLOONS

The first person in Ireland to fly in a hot air balloon was Richard Crosby from Ranelagh Gardens, Dublin, on 19 January 1785. Crosby dressed up for an attempt to cross the Irish Sea in a 'robe of oiled silk lined with white fur, waistcoast and breeches combined in one garment of quilted white satin, morocco boots and a montero cap of leopard skin'. Nevertheless, the first person to actually make it across by balloon, travelling from Portobello, Dublin, to Holyhead on 22 July 1817, was Windham Sadler. Sadler's father had tried the crossing in 1812 but came down in the sea.

    A gentleman whose balloon never made it into the sky was eccentric and recluse Benjamin O'Neill Stratford, the 6th and last Earl of Aldborough. Born in 1809, at Stratford Lodge near Baltinglass, the Earl spent some 20 years building a giant dirigible in an equally giant balloon house on his estate. Working like one possessed, he failed to keep a cook in employ and was instead supplied with meals by the Dublin mail coach which came daily. However, one Sunday morning in 1856, a fire broke out in the lodge and reduced the balloon house and dirigible to ashes. Defeated, the Earl retired to Alicante in Spain where he became such a recluse that he refused to have the dirty dishes collected after dinner from his suite, and instead moved from room to room as the leftovers accumulated in his wake.

### BALLYMAGASH

Village with petrol-pump-cum-grocery-shop at its centre, invented by one Frank Hall for his popular politico-satirical television series, *Hall's Pictorial Weekly*.

Also a slang word for the drug hashish. According to **Oliver St John Gogarty** in *As I was Going Down Sackville Street* (1937): 'Politics is the chloroform of the Irish People, or, rather, the hashish.' Perhaps this connection between politics and hashish is the root of the drug's nickname.

### BANBA

Ancient name for Ireland. Other common ones were Fodla and Eire.

The earliest known reference to Ireland comes in the writings of the Greek Stoic philosopher Poseidonios (*c.* 135–50 BC) who called it Ierne.

The term 'Emerald Isle' was probably first used by United Irishman William Drennan (1754–1820), a Belfast doctor practising in Dublin. His poem 'Erin' proclaims: 'Nor one feeling of vengeance presume to defile/The cause of the men of the Emerald Isle.'

### BANKING

The poet William Allingham (1824–89) was for a period a banker in Ballyshannon, Co. Donegal, where he is commemorated on a plaque outside the Bank of Ireland. It no longer seems to matter that he hated working in the bank, often said so, and left it to become a Customs Officer.

Someone else who hated banks was the customer who in 1992, according to the *Independent on Sunday*, dumped 20 tons of 'steaming horse manure on the steps of the Allied Irish Bank' in Cardiff, explaining: 'I want them to know what it is like when someone shits on you.'

A machine for printing and numbering bank notes was invented by Thomas Grubb who was born in Kilkenny in 1800.

### BARNACLE
Nora Barnacle was the object of **James Joyce**'s attentions.

According to Giraldus Cambrensis, or Gerald of Wales, who wrote an account of the history and topography of Ireland following two visits in the latter part of the 12th century, the barnacle goose reproduces without mating. For this reason the bishops and religious men of Ireland may eat it without sin during periods of fasting. Since it is not the progeny of flesh, it cannot be considered flesh itself. A secondary excuse suggests that the bird is in fact a type of fish.

(See **Tea**)

### BEAL NA MBLÁTH
The place in Co. Cork where **Michael Collins** was ambushed and killed on 22 August 1922. Beal na mBláth means the 'Mouth of Flowers'.

### BEAUTY
According to *Brewer's Dictionary of Phrase and Fable*, 3rd edition, an Irish Beauty was a woman with two black eyes – 'no uncommon "decoration" among the low Irish'. Thomas Heywood in his play *A Challenge for Beauty* (1636) has Manhurst say: 'I am cleane out of love with your Irish trowses [trousers]; they are for all the world like a jeaulous wife, always close at a

mans tayle' (III. vi).

Dublin-born writer and orator Edmund Burke (1729–97) entered Westminster in 1765, despite rumours that he was a closet Catholic, and all his life campaigned for Irish free trade and Catholic relief. His other great area of interest, however, was aesthetics and he is remembered for his enquiries into concepts of beauty. Burke died the year the creator of **Frankenstein** was born.

## BECKETT, SAMUEL (1906–90)

Arguably Ireland's most important playwright, poet and novelist. Tom Davies, in an article in the *Observer* in 1979, appeared not to agree, saying of Beckett's plays: 'They remind me of something Sir John Betjeman might do if you filled him up with benzedrine and then force-fed him intravenously with Guinness.'

Plays aside for a moment, Beckett, who was born on Good Friday, 13 April 1906, was employed by **James Joyce** in 1932 as his secretary, and also had the distinction of having received the Croix de Guerre for his activities with the French Resistance during World War II. However he was wounded in France on at least one occasion: in 1938 he survived a stabbing by a pimp and was found lying in a Paris street by the pianist Suzanne Deschevaux-Dumesnil, who married him 23 years later.

Beckett received the Nobel Prize for Literature in 1969, which must have been in recognition of his work as a playwright rather than as a novelist, because his novel *Murphy* was rejected by more than 40 publishers. However, Beckett, who was in Tunisia when the prize was announced, declined to travel to Stockholm to receive it.

## BEES

The first bees are said to have been introduced to Ireland from Wales in the 6th century by St Molagga, who set up his hives near the present town of Balbriggan. St Molagga's feast day is 20 January, which was the day in 1961 when John F. Kennedy was sworn in as President of the United States. Many Irish monasteries, as well as having the famous round towers, also had bee towers. The bee tower in the Cistercian monastery at Mellifont, for instance, was 40 foot tall.

St Gobnat is said to have used swarms of bees to attack her enemies.

(See **Bloom, Leopold**)

## BEHAN, BRENDAN (1923–64)

Dublin-born working-class playwright and poet, famous for *The Borstal Boy, The Quare Fellow,* and other works. His uncle was Peadar Kearney who wrote the words of the national anthem, 'The Soldier's Song' or *Amhrán na bhFiann,* which, in fact, is not an anthem but a march. The music was composed by Patrick Heney who died aged 30.

Behan's last words, to a nun, were reputedly: 'Thank you, Sister. May you be the mother of a bishop.' Behan's funeral was said to have been the biggest in Dublin since the death of **Michael Collins**.

## BERKELEY, GEORGE (1685–1753)

Bishop and philosopher who held, among other things, that objects existed only when they were perceived. Whether they exist or not, Berkeley, California, and its university, are named after him.

Berkeley also dabbled as a quack and it was he who reputedly caused Corny (Cornelius) Magrath, a youngster from Silvermines, Co. Tipperary, to grow to 7 foot by his 16th year. How Berkeley achieved this is not clear, but it is said the process involved the use of special baths. Magrath, however, left the bishop's care and went to Cork to join a wandering troupe which took him to Italy (where his portrait was painted by Pietro Longhi). After this he travelled to London and then back to Ireland where he died in 1759, aged 23. His corpse was stolen at his wake by students from Trinity College, who doped the mourners by putting laudanum in their whiskey. Quickly removed to the city centre college, the corpse was 'stripped down' before the relatives could do anything to prevent it, and the skeleton has remained in Trinity, going on exhibition there in 1992. Magrath had been, in fact, a mere 7 foot 2 inches.

Berkeley's other great interest was tar-water, which he recommended as a remedy for almost all known ailments. One of his books prompted the following reaction from Horace Walpole: 'The book contains every subject from tar-water to the trinity; however all the women read it and understand it no more than they would if it were intelligible.'

## BESTIALITY

Perhaps the most extraordinary account ever of a coronation is given by Giraldus Cambrensis in the 12th century. According to Cambrensis, it was the practice in Kenelcunill in 'the northern and farther part of Ulster' to anoint the new king in the following way. First of all a white mare was led into the middle of the court assembly, and the future king, in full view of his future subjects, would proceed to have sexual intercourse with her. Immediately following this, the mare was killed, chopped up into pieces and boiled, whereupon the water used in the boiling was then used to make a bath for the king-to-be. Once in the bath the future king had to eat and drink of the broth without recourse to his hands. When he had taken his fill he was carried from the bath and the coronation proper could begin.

(See **Cattle**)

## BETRAYAL

'Nobody can betray Ireland: it does not give him the chance; it betrays him first' – **Oliver St John Gogarty**, *As I was Going Down Sackville Street*, 1937.

## BETS

The word 'quiz' was coined in 1780 by a Dublin theatre manager by the name of Daly, who accepted a wager that he could not introduce a new word to the language. He achieved his purpose by scrawling the meaningless word on walls throughout the city, thereby guaranteeing that it would become a talking point.

It was also a bet that prompted the famous travels of Dubliner Thomas 'Buck' Whaley (1766–1800), eight years later, to walk from Dublin to Jerusalem and back within a year. The purse was £20,000 and Whaley was back, after a journey of some 7000 miles, in June 1789, with three months to spare. Typically he was afterwards reckless with his winnings and almost made a career out of being a self-ruined man.

## BILLY THE KID

A gun-toting cowboy with Irish blood otherwise known as William Bonney, otherwise known as Henry McCarty. Believed to have been born in New York, although it is possible he was born in Ireland, William, or Billy the Kid as he was better known, fought his fellow Irish-Americans as much as he did the Indians. The sheriff William Brady, the first man Billy killed, was an Irish-American, as was Pat Garrett, who eventually killed Billy on 15 July 1881, the year Pope John XXIII was born.

## BINGO

A form of gambling organized, in general, by religious communities.

## BLACK AND TANS

Notorious and undisciplined militia, recruited from British ex-servicemen fresh from the European front, which arrived in Ireland in 1920. The name was given its members because of their black and brown dress, a combination of police and military uniforms. Before this, Black and Tans had been the name of a famous pack of hounds. Nowadays it is the name given to an alcoholic drink combining Guinness stout and Smithwicks ale.

## BLACK EYES

(See **Marriage**)

## BLARNEY

Flattery, the Gift of the Gab, nonsense. So called after the famous castle in Co. Cork to which those seeking the 'gift of the gab' journey to kiss the celebrated Blarney Stone. The stone, which is approximately 4 foot long, 1 foot wide and 9 inches deep, is located over a drop of 120 feet, which does not seem to deter those who are set on leaving a trace of their saliva. As well as the inherent dangers of its position, there is also the unsavoury matter identified by Dave Allen: 'Only the Irish could persuade people to kiss a stone the Norman soldiers had urinated on.' Indeed, it is unknown how the kissing custom began, but a legend which offers one explanation for the origin of Blarney as insincere talk says that after a series of unfulfilled appointments between the Lord of Blarney (who was also the King of Munster) and Queen Elizabeth I, the Virgin Queen is reported to have dismissed the Lord's excuses as 'the usual Blarney'

The Irish love of talk has inspired many reactions. 'Every St Patrick's day every Irishman goes out to find another Irishman to make a speech to' – Shane Leslie, *American Wonderland,* 1936.

**BLINDNESS**
The most famous harper and composer of the 18th century, **Turlough Carolan** (1670–1738) was blind, as was the harper Denis O'Hempsey (1695–1807) who is reputed to have lived into his 111th year. Also blind were Anthony Raftery (1784–1835) the famous bard, and **Zozimus** (1794–1846) the Dublin street balladeer. How the Tyrone-born astronomer Thomas Maclear (1794–1879) managed to pursue his chosen profession despite going blind remains something of a mystery. The Irish surname O'Suilleabháin means 'one-eyed', while the Irish first name Síle (or Sheila) means blind. The noted Irish astronomer Sir Robert Ball (1840–1913) had only one eye after the other's removal in 1897. The artist Paul Henry (1876–1958), who is best remembered for his paintings of Achill, was colour-blind, and completely blind for the last 13 years of his life.

**BLOODY SUNDAY**
The name given to Sunday 30 January 1972, when thirteen unarmed civil rights demonstrators were shot dead by British troops in Derry.

**BLOOM, LEOPOLD**
The central character of *Ulysses*. Molly's cuckold husband and *aficionado* of the inner organs of beasts and fowl. His wife, Molly, once spoke in the region of 52,000 words without a stop. Leopold was stung by a bee in his garden on 23 May 1904.

(See **Liver**)

**BLOOMSDAY**
16 June 1904. The day on which the action of James Joyce's celebrated novel *Ulysses* takes place. It was on this day that Joyce and chambermaid Nora Barnacle first 'walked out' together.

According to the census taken in 1901, three years

before the events of the novel take place, the population of Dublin was a mere 290,638.

To mark Bloomsday in 1982, RTE radio broadcast an uninterrupted and unedited reading of *Ulysses* which began at 6.30 am and ended at 12.45 pm the following day.

## BODHRÁN

Upright drum made of goatskin, associated with traditional Irish music. Played with a double bulb-ended stick. Suspected etymological connection to the word *bodhar*, meaning 'deaf'.

A report in the *Evening Press* in November 1992 told of a nightclub doorman who was appearing before the Dublin Circuit Criminal Court after he allegedly had assaulted a young student. The report ends by saying that the student was left 'temporarily deaf in his left ear. The hearing continues.'

## BOG–TROTTER

Derogatory term for an Irish country person. The prologue to the anonymous English play, *The Royal Voyage* (1690), reads as follows: 'The next thing I'm to do you, to wit, is, that the End of this play is chiefly to expose the Perfidious, Base, Cowardly, Bloody Nature of the Irish, both in this and all past Ages, especially to give as lively a scheeme as will consist with what's past, so far of the word that Heathenish Barbarities committed by them on their peaceable British Neighbours, in that Bloody and Destestable Massacre and Rebellion of Forty-One, which will make the Nation stink as long as there's one Bog or Bog-Trotter left in it.' One scene of the play shows the barbarity of the bog-trotters who are standing about talking of all the dogs they've killed, burnt alive and made candles of. When they are confronted by English soliders, predictably they run away.

## BOLLIX

Testicles.

Also a negative answer to a request for anything, an enquiry about finances or any other conceivable kind of question.

Also: Poor Little Bollix – a term of affection.

An ironic piece of vandalism in 1961 left the winged angel over Oscar Wilde's grave in Paris without the aforementioned physical attributes. Action of a similar nature was taken against a work by artists Paki Smith and Ronan Halpin in Limerick in 1991 when their enormous and colourful piece of public sculpture, *The Wounded King*, lived up to its name, having its impact only partially reduced by nocturnal critics. The name Limerick, incidentally, means 'Bare Spot'.

## BOMBS

The Co. Mayo pilgrimage town of Knock, located close to the Atlantic seaboard, has an airport with an airstrip large enough for American B-52 bombers to refuel.

A bomber, this time German, which either purposely or by accident released its load on the Co. Wexford town of Campile, killed three young girls there in August 1940.

A similar incident in 1941 over Clontarf, Co. Dublin, killed 31 people and the compensation paid by the German government was used to build the notorious Ballymun flats in 1965.

## BONO (b. 1960)

Real name Paul Hewson. Lead singer with rock group **U2**, who attended University College Dublin for two weeks in September 1978 until it was discovered he didn't have the necessary admission qualifications.

(See **Virgins**)

**BOOK BURNING**
The first Irish writer to have his work publicly burned by the hangman in Dublin was John Toland (1670–1722), the book in question being *Christianity not Mysterious*, published ten years after Toland's conversion to Protestantism.

**BORDER**
Boundary which partitions parts of Ulster from other counties of the island and whose presence can best be detected by gauging petrol prices while driving between Monaghan and Fermanagh.

**BORSTAL BOY, THE**
Autobiographical account of the adventures of a would-be bomber, by the young **Brendan Behan**.

**BOUCICAULT, DION LARDNER (1820–90)**
Dublin-born author and playwright who wrote, among other plays, *The Colleen Bawn*. He was married three times, the third time bigamously, which caused a sensation and lost him many friends and admirers in his later years. However, he was undoubtedly consoled by the estimated $5 million he earned from his plays.

**BOXING**
Former WBA Featherweight Champion of the World Barry McGuigan comes from **Clones**, Co. Monaghan. He beat Eusebio Pedroza for the title in 1985, but lost it to Steve Cruz in 1986.

Ireland has produced 13 world boxing champions in all, although never a heavyweight. Four world heavyweight boxing champions, however, have had Irish parents: John L. Sullivan (1882–92), 'Gentleman

Jim' Corbett (1892–7), Gene Tunney (1926–8) and Jim Braddock (1935–7).

The famous legal battle which left Oscar Wilde branded a sodomite was against the Marquess of Queensberry, he who drew up the rules of boxing in 1867.

## BOYCOTT *v.*
'To send to Coventry'. After one Captain Boycott (1832–97), land agent to Lord Erne in Co. Mayo, who was ostracized in retaliation for evictions carried out under his orders. The word, in its present meaning, was first used by **Parnell** in Ennis, Co. Clare, in 1880 at a public meeting where he urged that there be imposed 'a moral Coventry'.

## BOYLE, ROBERT (1627–91)
Chemist and physicist.

(See **Urine**)

## BOYNE, BATTLE OF THE
On 1 July 1690, Catholics under James II were routed by Protestants under William of Orange. The Williamites then advanced on Limerick which was holding out under the command of Patrick Sarsfield but, despite a number of successful sorties from the besieged city, Sarsfield eventually surrendered in October 1691.

The River Boyne takes its name from Bóann, the goddess of the white cow.

(See **Mole**)

## BREHON LAWS
Ancient laws of Ireland, originating in the 3rd and prevailing until the 17th century. The position of jurist was hereditary, this seems somewhat unfair to modern critics. One bonus of the Brehon Laws, how-

ever, was that Irish women could keep their own names after marriage. Divorce was also permitted.

## BRENDAN, SAINT (*c.* AD 486–578)

'The Navigator'. Feast day 16 May. Irish monk born in Kerry and credited with the 'discovery' of America, possibly Iceland, Greenland and a few other places besides, some 900 years before Columbus. The evidence for this claim comes from his book *Navagatio* in which he describes his travels. However, at least until 1977, it was thought by many that the beautiful Land of Promise in the Atlantic to which he voyaged may have been, in fact, nothing more remote than the Canary Islands. Many found it impossible to believe that Brendan could have crossed the Atlantic in the small craft known as a currach, as it is claimed. In June 1977, however, Tim Severin, with a crew of three, traversed the 2000-mile stretch between Ireland and Newfoundland in a rigger made of ox-hide on a wooden frame, showing that it is indeed possible, if not probable, that 'The Navigator' story is true.

Another boat to have crossed the Atlantic, albeit one of a completely different class, was the *Gypsy Moth*, in which Sir Francis Chichester single-handedly made the crossing in 1966–7. It was built in Arklow.

## BRENNAN

A common Irish surname. One who brands the hands of criminals or one who is so branded.

(See **Submarines**)

## BRIAN BORU (940–1014)

The most famous of the legendary High Kings of Ireland was Brian MacKennedy, known as Brian Boru (Brian of the Tributes). Actually, for someone so famous, he was something of a late starter, not becoming king until he was 61 years of age. Nevertheless his reign was not without its moments.

He gave the Vikings a hard time when he had the opportunity, and he is credited as the first of the High Kings to exploit the idea of a navy – although the Irish were a maritime people long before him. Somewhat pathetically, however, he was killed in his changing tent while saying the rosary in thanksgiving after the Battle of Clontarf on Good Friday, 23 April 1014.

(See **Gout**)

## BRIGID, SAINT (AD 452–523)

A popular woman saint who was probably born at Faughart near Dundalk. She is said to have transformed her bathwater into beer for visiting clerics, which no doubt added to her popularity. Her feast day (1 February), the first day of spring, suggests that Brigid is actually part of the native Irish pantheon, and long predates the coming of Christianity. The day is marked, not by the taking of baths or by drinking to excess, though it is not prohibited to do so, but by the more leisurely making from rushes or straw of St Brigid's Crosses. Brigid died and was buried at Kildare but her remains were exhumed and removed to Downpatrick for burial near those of **St Patrick**.

(See **Cattle**)

## BRITAIN

The United Kingdom of Great Britain and Northern Ireland comprises England, Scotland, Wales and Northern Ireland, though the Republic of Ireland still maintains a claim to the northern counties. The distance between the two islands that may or may not make up the British Isles is at one point just 13 miles (British miles, that is, the Irish version being 480 yards longer).

## BRIXTON

South London area in Lambeth Borough. The Lord Mayor of Cork, Terence MacSwiney, died on hunger strike in prison there in 1920. MacSwiney's funeral took place in the cathedral at Southwark, arousing much debate as to whether he should be admitted into a Catholic church after such a death. The Catholic Bishop of London who faced the controversy and granted MacSwiney a proper funeral was named, suitably, Dr Amigo.

## BROGUE

The Irish for shoe. Also the Irish dialect of the English language. Brogues as a form of clothing were originally garments which were both trousers and shoes, all in one. So when **Shakespeare** says in *Cymbeline*, 'And put my clouted brogues from off my feet', he seems to be asking that his pants be taken off as well.

When Joan FitzGerald, wife of the ex-Fine Gael leader Garret FitzGerald, stepped in to defend her husband during an election campaign by saying 'It was my fault. I'm to blame,' she was referring to the fact that her husband had gone out in public wearing odd shoes.

## BROTHERS, CHRISTIAN

(See **Rice, Edmund Ignatius**; **Pineapples**; **Submarines**)

## BROWN, CHRISTY (1932–81)

Dublin-born working-class novelist and poet, one of 21 children of whom only 13 survived infancy. Despite suffering from cerebral palsy, Brown became an internationally celebrated author with his autobiography *My Left Foot* (1954), later the subject of a film starring Daniel Day-Lewis. His *Down All the Days* (1970) was translated into 14 languages.

Another poet who died in 1981 was the MP for Fermanagh and South Tyrone, Bobby Sands, who died on 11 April on a mass hunger strike that also claimed the lives of nine fellow prisoners in the Maze prison. Cuban leader Fidel Castro, perhaps aware of the literary connection, said of the strikers: 'The Irish patriots are in the process of writing one of the most heroic pages in human history.'

## BUENOS AIRES STANDARD

South America's first English-language newspaper, published by Dublin-born Michael G. Mulhall (b. 1936). The first publication that might be called a newspaper was *An Account of the Chief Occurances of Ireland*. Produced in 1659, it ran for five issues. The first Irish magazine, however, was produced in New York in 1810 and was called *The Shamrock or Hibernian Chronicle*.

## BULLET

A projectile fired from a gun. Garrett Mór Fitzgerald (the Mór means 'big'), who was Earl of Kildare, was, in 1513, the first recorded victim of a shooting in Ireland.

Bullet is also a popular game in Cork and Armagh. It is played on country roads with a metal ball of 28 ounces which is thrown over a predetermined course in the least possible number of throws. Between country and city roads, there are approximately 57,000 miles of potential bullet-playing areas in Ireland.

## BULLSHIT

Nonsense, lies, exaggeration. The word 'bull' was originally applied to the kind of nonsense stage Irishmen spoke on the English stage. A play from 1690 by W.J. Lawrence, for example, had the following title and subtitle: *Teagueland Jests, or Bog Witticism. In Two Parts. The first being a Compleat Collection of the most learned Bulls, Elaborate Quibbles, and Wise Sayings of Teagueland till the year 1688. The Second contains many Comical Stories and famous Blunders of those*

*Dear joys since the late King James landing among them.*

## BUNGALOW

Jack Fitzsimons, author of *Bungalow Bliss* (1971) and popularizer of the pre-designed, off-the-rack look of rural Irish houses of the last 20 years, once said: 'The new generation in the countryside would rather own an American homestead in Ireland than pine for an Irish homestead in America.'

## BURIAL

Mr Samuel Grubb, a Quaker who died in the 1920s, is buried in a standing position, 2144 feet up the north slope of the Sugar Loaf mountain in Co. Wicklow.

In 1968, Mike Meaney from Ballyporeen, Co. Tipperary, was voluntarily buried alive in a coffin underneath Butty Sugrue's public house in Kilburn, North London, for a total of 61 days.

One Francis Tuckey, writing in 1753, tells of a burial in Cork: 'Francis Taylor was buried in St Peter's church yard, and the next morning was found sitting up in the grave, one of his shoulders much mangled, one of his hands full of clay, and blood running from his eyes, a melancholy instance of the fatal consequences of a too precipitate internment.'

There is an account from the 12th century which tells of an island in the sea off Connaught, consecrated by St Brendan, where corpses need not be buried but are left in the open where they remain without corruption.

(See **Reincarnation**)

## BURKE, EDMUND (1729–97)

(See **Beauty**)

## CAMELS

The wild camels in Central Australia are the descendants of those introduced to the continent by a team of explorers who set out to cross from south to north, led by Galway-born Robert O'Hara Burke (1820–61), who died with his partner Wills in the attempt. Their only surviving companion, John King, was found and cared for by aborigines and was finally reached by a relief expedition in September 1861.

Two Irishmen who escaped death in Australia, this time by execution and not on account of camels, were Michael Ireland and Morris Lyene. They went on to become Attorneys General.

## CAROLAN, TURLOUGH (1670–1738)

Blind and illiterate Meath-born harper and composer of the famous *Carolan's Concerto*. Among his other tunes was the air that became 'The Star-Spangled Banner'. Always fond of the drink, on his death bed, according to **Oliver Goldsmith**, he asked that a cup of *uisce beatha* (whiskey) be brought to him. In the event he was unable to drink it but 'observed with a smile that it would be hard if two such friends as he and the cup should part, at least without kissing, and then expired.' A skull in the National Museum, which was given over by the Masonic Lodge, is reputedly that of the harper.

## CARRAUNTOOHILL
The highest mountain in Ireland at 3414 feet.

## CARSON, EDWARD (1854–1935)
The man who spent his life trying to keep Ulster part of the United Kingdom was actually born in Harcourt Street in Dublin, though his mother was Isabella Lambert whose ancestor, General Lambert, had been one of **Oliver Cromwell**'s major-generals.

(See **Wilde, Oscar**)

## CASEY, BISHOP EAMONN (b. 1927)
One-time Bishop of Galway who in 1992 was revealed to be the father of a child by his second cousin, Annie Murphy, a revelation which led to his resignation and despatch by the Vatican to an undisclosed location in the US. In a 1971 interview Bishop Casey had said: 'There is far greater need for parents to be available to their children than previously.'

## CASHEL, ROCK OF
Cormac's Chapel in Cashel is interesting in that, unusually among Irish churches, it has no west doorway. The Rock of Cashel itself is said to be a piece of rock from the Devil's Bit which the devil dropped from his mouth in shock on spying St Patrick setting up a church in the area. It is also the place Patrick is said to have explained the Trinity through the symbol of the shamrock. St Dympna is the patron saint of people possessed by the devil, which seems to be something of a contradiction as who, if possessed by the devil, would turn to a saint.

(See **Ice**)

## CATERPILLAR TRACKS

Castlecomer, Co. Kilkenny man John Walken was responsible for the invention of caterpillar tracks for heavy vehicles in 1899.

## CATTLE

Until the end of 1993 when she died, the oldest cow in the world, at 49 years, was Big Bertha who lived on the farm of Jerome O'Leary near Kenmare in Co. Kerry. Through appearances at shows, Bertha, who was born on St Patrick's Day in 1944, had managed to raise more than £50,000 for charities including cancer research. At the time of her death, while O'Leary was considering sending her to a taxidermist, Bertha's oldest surviving offspring was a mere 35 years of age.

Approximately 3999 cows more than Bertha were given by Rory O'Connor, High King of Ireland, to the Norse army which he had defeated at Blanchardstown near Dublin in an attempt to compensate them for their disappointment. The ages of the cows were not, however, recorded.

In 1992 there were 6,073,000 cows in Ireland, a good percentage of them presumably the relations of a Friesian bull by the name of Bendalls Adema which, before dying at Clondalkin, Dublin, on 8 November 1978, had sired an estimated 212,000 progeny by artificial insemination.

**St Brigid**, busy woman, is the patron saint of dairy workers.

St Columcille banned cows from near his monasteries on the grounds that where there are cows there are women, and where there are women there's temptation.

According to a letter of the time to Rome, priests in the 17th century had to supplement their small incomes with cattle-dealing. In January 1994, an article in the *Sunday Tribune* broke the news of a new method. An organization called CLASS, or Central Livestock Auction Satellite Sales, had begun the setting up of a once-weekly broadcast 'beamed into farms and slaughterhouses equipped with a satellite dish' so as to enable live auctions to be conducted from the comfort of home.

According to Giraldus Cambrensis, in 1174 a man was seen in Wicklow who, instead of having feet and hands, had the hooves of an ox. About the same period Cambrensis relates that a cow gave birth to a man-cow in the mountains around Glendalough, following a man's having intercourse with her, a practice which Cambrensis calls 'a particular vice of that people'.

(See **Goldsmith, Oliver**; **Boyne, Battle of the**; **Fairy Forts**; **Amputation**)

### CAVAN
North midland county and town, only an hour from Dublin. Cavan means 'hollow'.

### CELTS
The Celts, so the story goes, arrived in Ireland around 700 BC from central Europe. They lived in ring forts and divided the land up into five provinces, Ulster, Leinster, Meath, Munster and Connaught, with their High King being located in the ancient pagan site of **Tara** in Meath. That's one version. Another, more credible one, is that the Celts, as such, did not actually exist, and that what is seen to have been the influence of a single invading force is in fact a more gradual and scattered influence of various European and Mediterranean peoples who may possibly have spoken a common language. Some have gone so far as to claim that the Celts were the invention of **Eamon de Valera** in his bid to find an Irish identity after independence.

## CEMENT

Cement was invented by Sligoman Bryan Higgins and patented on 18 January 1779 (British Patent No. 1207).

The smallest church in Ireland, dedicated to St Gobnan, is only 10 foot by 6 foot. St Gobnan is the patron saint of builders.

## CHANGELINGS

It was a very popular belief in former times that the forces of evil could substitute a changeling for a natural child. In May 1884 the *Daily Telegraph* carried a report on the arrest in Clonmel of two women who had put a child, naked, onto a hot shovel 'under the impression that this would break the charm'. The child suffered severe burns.

## CHESS

Board game popular in Ireland since pre-Christian times, proficiency at which was reputedly one of the entry requirements to the warrior band, the **Fianna**.

## CHRISTMAS

Someone who may have been playing Father Christmas when he met his death was Waterford-born painter Michael Angelo Hayes (1820–77) who drowned aged 57 on 31 December when he mysteriously fell into a tank of water on the roof of his house at Salem Place in Dublin.

(See **Purcell, Noel**)

## CHURCHILL, SIR WINSTON (1874–1965)

English politician who was born in the ladies' cloakroom of Blenheim Palace to a mother who was one-eighth Iroquois Indian. It was Churchill who urged Lloyd George to opt for 'a tremendous onslaught' against the troublesome Irish in 1920, adding, on another occasion, 'We have always found the Irish a bit odd. They refuse to be English.' As a young man Churchill was a regular visitor to Castle Leslie in Co. Monaghan where is kept, among other things, the original pen with which Pope Pius IX signed the Dogma of the Immaculate Conception, and a harp belonging to the poet William Wordsworth, who was also a visitor to the home of the novelist Maria Edgeworth (1767–1849) in nearby Longford. Edgeworth's father, Richard Lovell Edgeworth, who had decided to come to Ireland rather than be an absentee landlord, was the father of 22 children and was four times married before he died at the age of 73. Churchill himself survived to the age of 91, dying on 20 January, exactly 70 years to the day after his father Randolph. Maria Edgeworth was born on the first day of 1767.

(See **CúChulainn**)

## CLADDAGH
Small area in Galway city where the famous Claddagh ring originates. The heart on the ring is worn pointing out towards the fingers when the wearer is betrothed, and in when the wearer is married. The Claddagh was once an Irish-speaking haven in an almost wholly Norman county.

## CLAIRVOYANTS
People who can see into the future. **St Malachy** (*c.* 1096–1148) predicted he would die at Clairvaux in France, which he did, on All Souls' Day, 2 November 1148. The word 'clairvoyant' comes from the name of the town. Malachy also predicted that there would be only two more popes after the present John Paul II.

The Tullamore, Co. Offaly writer Elliot Warburton, who died in a fire on the steamer *Amazon* on 4 January 1852, wrote a novel *Darien, or the Merchant Prince*, in which is described such a maritime disaster. His book appeared posthumously.

## CLEW BAY
Bay on the coast of Mayo in which, it is said, there are 365 islands, one for every day of the year.

## CLIFDEN
One of the prettiest towns in Ireland, which was devised and built by a local landlord, John D'Arcy, in 1819. It was near here that Alcock and Brown crash-landed in 1919 after their history-making transatlantic crossing.

## CLONES
The birthplace of people who look like the local-born boxer Barry McGuigan.

(See **Boxing**)

## COINS
The Irish have a great affection for animals, witnessed by the appearance of a variety of creatures on their coins. The suggestion for this came in 1926 from **William Butler Yeats**, then Senator, and the coins were designed by Percy Metcalf. People refer to the side of the coin on which the animals are depicted as being 'heads' while the side with the harp is known as 'tails' because the head of the ruling monarch had formerly appeared in place of the animals.

The first coins minted in Ireland were in 1005 by the Norse king, Sitric III. The first coins to feature the head of an English monarch were those in the reign of King John, who reigned from 1199–1216. Viking and North African coins were found in Dunmore Cave near Kilkenny during excavations in 1967. Also found were the skeletons of 44 women and children. It is thought they had hidden down there to avoid the Vikings in AD 928 and got lost or trapped there.

(See **Harp**)

### COLLINS, MICHAEL (1890–1922)

'The Big Fellow'. Founder and Commander-in-Chief of the Irish Army, Michael Collins was born near Clonakilty in Co. Cork. He is generally recognized as being the originator of the concept of guerilla warfare and it was his tactics which were responsible for the smashing of the British Army's intelligence network in Dublin. A signatory to the Treaty of 1921, Collins was ambushed and killed in 1922 by those opposed to the controversial settlement, and almost immediately entered the ranks of mythological Irish heroes. As one of those who took part in the Dublin uprising in the **GPO** in 1916, Collins was probably the best qualified to be there, having worked as a post office clerk for nine years in the London borough of Kensington.

(See **Gandhi, Mohandâs K.**)

### COLOURFUL CLERGY

Frederick Hervey (1730–1803), Church of Ireland Bishop of Derry, often visited Rome where he dressed in red plush breeches and a broad-brimmed white hat and was confused with a Catholic. His brother Augustus wed one Miss Chudleigh, wearing the ring of a bed curtain. In 1750 the Church of Ireland Bishop of Raphoe was shot dead while attempting to carry out a highway robbery, and, some 50-odd years before, a Bishop of Derry died from an accident said to have taken place during his attempt to burn a statue of the Virgin Mary.

### COLUM, PADRAIC (1881–1972)

Longford-born railway clerk, dramatist and poet who was responsible for the swing from Celtic mythology to peasant reality in plays produced at the Abbey

Theatre, where he was the last survivor of the founding generation of writers. He is perhaps best remembered for his lyrics which included 'She Moved Through the Fair'.

(See **Ukelele**)

## COLUMBA, SAINT (AD 521–597)

(See **Resurrection**; **Nessie**; **Rats**)

## COMMITMENTS, THE

Internationally hyped Alan Parker movie of the Roddy Doyle (b. 1958) book of the mythical northside Dublin soul band of the same name.

## COMMON BUTTERWORTH

Violet-coloured wild flower. One of Ireland's only insectivorous (insect-eating) plants.

## COMMUNISM

Friedrich Engels (1820–95), the German socialist who founded Communism with Karl Marx, believed that the Irish supplied 'England, America, Australia, etc. with prostitutes, casual labourers, pimps, thieves, swindlers, beggars and other rabble'. Marx was, however, reputedly an admirer of William Thompson (1775–1883), a wealthy landlord from Cork, who was commemorated by a bust in the International Communist Museum in Prague. Thompson, who professed to being a believer in Communism and female emancipation, and who spoke out regularly in their support, had a somewhat misguided vision which can be best understood by his insistence on feeding his pigs with sawdust after learning that all animals, flesh and bones, contain the same basic minerals as wood. After his death his body was dug up (at his own request) to be put on show, and though he had asked that his skeleton be tipped with silver paint, being keen 'to present a fashionable appearance', his remains were certainly not taken to Red Square in Moscow.

According to the Rev. Ian Paisley, 'The Roman Catholic Church is getting nearer to communism every day' (1969).

The lyrics of 'The Red Flag' are by Co. Meath man Jim Connell.

(See **Moscow**)

## CONDOM

Generally available until its withdrawal in 1936, the condom was more recently at the centre of an enormous debate after its proposed reintroduction. In 1974 **Oliver J. Flanagan**, TD, explaining his vote against its reintroduction then, said: 'It is a vote against filth and dirt... Coupled with the chaotic drinking we have, the singing bars, lounge bars, the side-shows and all-night shows, the availability of condoms will, in my opinion, add more serious consequences to those already there. You do not quench a fire by sprinkling it with petrol.'

In 1991 one record store attempting to retail condoms directly to the public in its Dublin city centre outlet was restrained by a Court Order. However, condoms were made generally available in 1992.

## CONGO

26 Irish soldiers died (not all in action) in the Congo in the years 1960–4.

The Rev. Henry Grattan Guinness (1835–1910) was an evangelist who published a grammar of the Congo language.

## CONNOLLY, JAMES (1868–1916)

Born in the Edinburgh slum of Cowgate, Connolly did not come to Ireland until he was 28, and in 1903 he went to the United States for seven years where in 1905 he helped found the International Workers of the World, otherwise known as the 'Wobblies'. In 1910 he returned to Ireland to lead, with Larkin, the workers in the great lockout of 1913. Which meant that he spent in all only 13 years in Ireland before being executed while sitting in a chair, too weak to stand.

## CONRADH NA GAEILGE

The Irish League, not to be confused with the League of Ireland, was founded in 1893 with the aim of reviving the Irish language, which was seen, even then, to be in decline.

## CONTRADICTION

The Irish have long been experts in the art of contradiction and paradox. For many this is seen as an attractive quality, while for others... 'A fighting race who never won a battle, a race of politicians who cannot govern themselves, a race of writers without a great one of native strain, an island race who have yet to man a fleet for war, for commerce, or for the fishing banks and to learn how to build ships, a pious race excelling in blasphemy, who feel most wronged by those they have first injured, who sing of love and practise fratricide, preach freedom and enact suppressions, a race of democrats who sweat the poor, have a harp for an emblem and no musicians, revelled on foreign gold and cringed without it, whose earlier history is myth and murder, whose later, murder, whose tongue is silver and whose heart is black, a race skilled in idleness, talented in hate, inventive only in slander, whose land is a breeding-ground of modern reaction and the cradle of western crime' – Tom Penhaligon, *The Impossible Irish*, 1935.

## CORONATION
(See **Gout**; **Bestiality**)

## CRABS
It was following a meal of crabs that Bram Stoker had the nightmare which gave him the idea for ***Dracula***.

## CREATION
The Creation of the world took place on 23 October 4004 BC, according to James Ussher (1581–1656), Archbishop of Armagh, historian and theologian, who is chiefly remembered for his radical system of chronology. The year after Ussher was born (1582) had ten days removed from it by Pope Gregory in order to bring the calendar back into line with the sun, so that Ussher lived ten days less than we might suppose. Presumably he took this into account when making other calculations.

## CROAGH PATRICK
Mountain in Mayo, the site of annual pilgrimages in July by travellers in bare feet. It was here that St Patrick was said to have sounded his bell, at which interruption all the snakes in Ireland gathered and threw themselves over the precipice and into the sea for ever.

An electric bell was invented in 1833 by one A.H. McGauley and given the unlikely name of the Trembler Interrupter.

## CROMWELL, OLIVER (1599–1658)
Lord Protector. Infamous English officer responsible for a particularly bloody campaign in Ireland on his arrival in 1649, which included the slaughter of 16,000 citizens of Wexford. By 1660 one-quarter of the Catholic population was dead. Thousands were deported or sold as slaves to the West Indies, an estimated 12,000 having arrived there by the end of the

decade. Still on a morbid note, two years after his death, Cromwell's body was exhumed and decapitated, the head placed on a spike outside Westminster from where it was reputedly blown off in 1685 and after which it remained in private possession until 1960, when it was purchased by his old college, Sidney Sussex in Cambridge.

(See **Marvell, Andrew**; **Treaty, The**; **Warts**)

## CROWN JEWELS

The Irish Crown Jewels were stolen in July 1907 from the Bedford Tower of Dublin Castle and have never since been seen.

When the British Crown Jewels were stolen in 1671, the thief, an Irish adventurer by the name of Colonel Thomas Blood, was given a full pardon by Charles II. Blood had been apprehended while trying to barter his loot in an alehouse.

## CRUMLIN

Dublin suburb designed in the shape of the eucharistic cross because building started during the Eucharistic Congress of 1932.

## CÚCHULAINN

2nd- or 3rd-century warrior, hurler and traveller, and subsequently mythological hero whose blood was drunk by a raven. CúChulainn earned his name by killing the ferocious hound of Culainn, *cú* being the Irish word for 'hound'. Though mortally wounded, he managed to defend the Gap of Ulster against invading enemies by tying himself to an upright post.

Patrick Sarsfield, Earl of Lucan, was mortally wounded in 1693 and said: 'Oh that this were for Ireland,' but it was of CúChulainn that a bronze likeness was made for Dublin's General Post Office. The statue was the work of Oliver Sheppard (1865–1941), and the head was modelled on the artist James Sleator who taught painting to **Winston Churchill** in London.

## CULDEES

'Companions of God'. Called after St Aengus (*c.* AD 824) who was known as *Céile Dé*, and who lived for a time in monasteries in Laois and Tallaght, the Culdees were a religious community following the rule of the Archbishop of Metz, who arrived in Ireland at the end of the 8th century. Among their practices was the recommendation of 365 prayers, 365 genuflexions and 365 'blows of the scourge' every day for a year so that a soul could be rescued from hell. Not surprisingly, the Culdees had ceased to exist by the 14th century.

## CURRACH

Small fishing vessel used off the west coast, traditionally leather over a wooden frame.

(See **Brendan, Saint**)

## DA

Common form of address from son to father.

Also a movie from the Hugh Leonard (b. 1923) play of the same name, starring Martin Sheen. Despite this and numerous novels, plays and contributions to Irish letters, Leonard, whose real name is Jack Keyes Byrne, is among the writers who is not among the writers included in the controversial three-volume *Field Day Anthology of Irish Writing*. In his case, uniquely, he declined the invitation.

## DÁIL ÉIREANN

Irish for 'House of Parliament'. The present building in Dublin is the former home of the Duke of Leinster. The first meeting of the Dáil was held in Dublin's Mansion House in 1919, and it was here that the adoption of the Declaration of Independence and the signing of the Truce took place in 1921.

## DARKNESS

Dunmore Cave in Co. Kilkenny, also known as *Dearc Fearna,* is reputedly one of Ireland's darkest places.

(See **Coins**)

## DE VALERA, EAMON (1882–1975)

Popularly known as 'Dev' or 'The Long Fellow', de Valera was 6 foot 3 inches of American-born republican who became President of Ireland for 14 years, retiring at the age of 90. Described by **Oliver St John Gogarty** as 'the Spanish onion in the Irish stew', de Valera was born in the same year as **James Joyce** and came to Ireland with his grandmother to live in Bruree, Co. Limerick. De Valera went from being the last prisoner in Dublin's Kilmainham Gaol when he was freed on 16 July 1924 to founding the **Fianna Fáil** party in 1926 and the *Irish Press* newspaper in 1931. This shaper of the Irish mind and father of the Free State and the independent Republic was also bestowed with the Order of Christ by Pope John XXIII.

Something of de Valera's vision of Ireland can be seen in the following famous extract from a St Patrick's Day radio broadcast in 1943 where he looked forward to 'a land whose countryside would be bright with cosy homesteads, whose fields and villages would be joyous with the sounds of industry, with the romping of sturdy children, the contests of athletic youths and the laughter of comely maidens, whose firesides would be forums for the wisdom of serene old age.' To this end he put paid to traditional dance meetings at the crossroads with the Public Dance Halls Act of 1935 which insisted that all such gatherings take place indoors.

(See **Emergency**; **Sexy**; **Xanthodont**)

## DEAD, THE

The last story in Joyce's *Dubliners*, adapted in what was to be director John Huston's last film.

## DERRY

The older name of the city now often known, particularly among the Unionist community, as Londonderry.

The name Derry comes from *doire* meaning 'oakwood'. The city grew up around a monastery founded by St Columba in AD 546. It was besieged by the armies of James II for 105 days in 1689, but its defenders held out. During this siege the Rev. George Walker, the Protestant Bishop of Derry, is believed to have first issued the call 'No Surrender', now the rallying cry of Ulster Unionists. On 13 April 1829, the day the Parliament of the United Kingdom granted the vote to Irish Catholics, a statue of Walker on the Walls of Derry collapsed.

In 1938 the electoral boundaries of Derry were redrawn so that 9600 nationalist electors returned eight councillors while 7500 unionist electors returned twelve.

The song, 'All Kinds of Everything', which won the 1970 Eurovision Song Contest was sung by Derry-born Dana (real name Rosemary Brown). The first name of one of its co-writers was Derry (Lindsay).

## DESIRE
A song by U2 that made No.1 in the UK charts.

The Irish name Connor (Conchúr) means 'high desire'.

## DEVIL
A statement by Irish bishops in 1933 on the phenomenon of all-night dances read: 'During the intervals the devil is busy; yes, very busy, as sad experience proves, and on the way home in the small hours of the morning, he is busier still.'

It was widely believed in former times that the rook and the raven had three drops of the devil's blood in them.

(See **Cashel, Rock of**)

## DEVLIN, BERNADETTE (MCALISKEY) (b. 1947)

Twenty-one years old when she was elected on 17 April 1969, Bernadette Devlin became the youngest MP at Westminster, the youngest woman ever there and the youngest MP elected on universal suffrage. Referred to by British politician Stratton Mills as 'Fidel Castro in a miniskirt', Devlin was arrested in 1969 for inciting the 'Battle of the Bogside', for which she was sentenced to six months' imprisonment on 22 November. In 1981 she survived an assassination attempt when she was shot by Loyalist gunmen.

## DICKENS, CHARLES (1812–70)

English novelist famous for his character portraits. Despite the fact that he must have frequently met members of the huge Irish community in England during his lifetime, in all his 17 novels there is not a single Irish character. However, this is not to suggest that Dickens had no admiration for the Irish. After meeting two Irish emigrants in New York during the Famine, he said: 'It would be hard to keep your modern republics going without the countrymen and countrywomen of these two labourers.'

## DIET

One of the main traditional foods on the island is, of course, the potato. The harpist Denis O'Hempsey (1695–1807), for one, professed to live on a diet that consisted only of milk, potatoes and water, and he lived in three different centuries. An Irish boy of 16 years who was discovered in 1672 and found to be dumb, was thought to have been raised by sheep in the style of Romulus and Remus. It is said that his diet consisted solely of hay and grass and his sole form of communication was a kind of bleating.

Perhaps one of the strangest eating habits associated with Ireland is that of the eels who arrive here from their breeding grounds in the Sargasso Sea, having taken about two and a half years to make the journey. When they arrive, they swim up the rivers and streams, eating as they go, but nevertheless it takes them about ten years to reach even half a pound weight. Then, suddenly, they stop growing and feeding. In fact the following autumn they retrace their steps, so to speak, and head again for the good old Sargasso Sea, without ever eating again in their lives, which seems an extreme reaction to Irish cuisine.

(See **Bloom, Leopold**; **Swift, Jonathan**)

## DOLMENS
Stone formations unique to the Celtic countries, formed by three uprights and one horizontal. Thought to have been used as burial stones. The most famous dolmen is Poulnabrone in the Burren (Ir. *boireann*, 'rocky land') of Co. Clare, but the largest, weighing about 100 tons, is Browne's Hill in Co. Carlow.

Dolmen Press: an important literary publishing house founded by the late Liam Miller.

## DONNE, JOHN
English poet who wrote in 'Loves Warre', *c*. 1594: 'Sick Ireland is with a strange warre possest/like to an Ague; now raging, now at rest;/which time will cure: yet it must doe her good/if she were purg'd, and her head vayne let blood.'

## DRACULA
Vampire creation of Dubliner **Bram Stoker**. In his *Famous Imposters* (1910) Stoker suggests that **Queen Elizabeth I** may have been a man in disguise.

## DRINK
Liquid with alcohol content.

In his *Life on the Mississippi* (1883), the American

author Mark Twain relates a meeting with an
Irishman who explains why the Irish supposedly are
not fond of beer. 'They don't drink it, sir. They can't
drink it, sir. Give an Irishman lager for a month, and
he's a dead man. An Irishman is lined with copper,
and the beer corrodes it. But whiskey polishes the
copper, and is the saving of him, sir.' Brendan Behan,
however, had a strict rule about drinking: 'I only take
a drink on two occasions – when I'm thirsty and when
I'm not.'

Another writer, Sean O'Faolain, once suggested:
'An Irish queer is a fellow who prefers women to
drink.'

Irish priests obviously preferred drink to women,
to such an extent that Oliver Plunkett was once
caused to remark: 'Give me an Irish priest without
this vice and he is assuredly a saint.'

J.P. Donleavy (b. 1926) is the author of, among
many bestselling novels, *The Ginger Man*, in which
appears the following: 'When I die I want to decom-
pose in a barrel of porter and have it served in all the
pubs in Dublin.' *The Ginger Man*, incidentally, has the
distinction of having been banned, not just once, but
twice – first in 1956 and again in 1969.

(See **Brigid, Saint**; **Carolan, Turlough**)

## DRUIDS

The druids, according to the historian Pliny, measured their ages as if they had all been born on the
fifth day of the moon which was therefore always a
sacred day. It was from the druids that we adopted
mistletoe as a special symbol for the feast of
Christmas. Again according to Pliny, the druids also
ate human flesh, but this is disputed by some histori-
ans who argue that they merely sacrificed humans
but did not actually consume them.

### DUBLIN (BAILE ÁTHA CLIATH)
The capital of Ireland, Dublin was reputedly visited by St Patrick in AD 448 and converted to Christianity. The marauding Vikings landed here in AD 841 (though the millennial celebrations of the founding of the city were inexplicably held in 1988, 39 years too late) and they managed to hang on until **Brian Boru** defeated them at the Battle of Clontarf in 1014. In 1172 Henry II granted the city to the men of Bristol in a charter.

### DUBLINERS
James Joyce's famous collection of short stories.

### DUBLINERS, THE
Ronnie Drew's (b. 1934) famous collection of instrument-playing, mostly bearded musicians.

### DUDE
The word 'dude' is believed to have been invented to describe Chester Alan Arthur (1830–86), the US President whose father came from Cullybackey in Co. Antrim.

### DUNPHY, EAMON
Former footballer.

### EARLS, FLIGHT OF THE
Famous hasty departure of the Donegal earls O'Neill
and O'Donnell to Spain in 1607, seen as the end of
hope for Irish self-rule. Their flight followed the Battle
of Kinsale in 1601, at which some 2000 on the Irish
side, and a single soldier on the enemy side, perished.
The Earls stopped off *en route* to ensure themselves
good luck by visiting the relic of the true cross at Holy
Cross Abbey in Co. Tipperary.

### EASTER RISING
The rebellion of 1916. 'The Forces of the Irish
Republic which was proclaimed in Dublin on Easter
Monday, 24 April, have been in possession of the cen-
tral part of the capital since 12 noon on that day,'
read **Patrick Pearse**'s statement.

Possibly because it was organized by poets and
others who were keenly aware of the impact of language, much of the symbolism of the Easter Rising
centred around the Proclamation of the new Republic.
One of the first acts of the rebels, therefore, was to
break into a shop for nails with which to hang the
posters announcing independence.

While the takeover of the GPO was going on, a raid for guns and ammunition was also underway at the Magazine Fort in the Phoenix Park, and it was here that the first fatality of the Rising occurred. The 17-year-old son of the Fort's commanding officer was shot dead as he ran to raise the alarm.

## ELECTRO-CARDIOGRAPH MACHINE
Invented by Dubliner Lucien Bull in 1908.

## ELECTRON
The first use of the word 'electron' in its present meaning is attributed to Irishman George Johnstone Stoney in 1891.

## ELEPHANT
Possibly one of the most interestingly entitled pamphlets to appear in 17th-century Ireland was *An anatomical account of the Elephant accidentally burnt in Dublin on June 17, 1681...*

(See **Nudity**)

## ELIZABETH I, QUEEN (1533–1603)
Queen of England and Ireland from 1558 to 1603 who, on his return after seven years travelling, forgave Edward de Vere, the Earl of Oxford, for an earlier indiscretion. 'My Lord,' she said, 'I had forgot the Fart.'

(See **Blarney**; **Dracula**)

## EMERGENCY
The term used by the neutral Irish for World War II.

In 1941, it was suggested by Adolf Hitler that the 25th anniversary of the 1916 Rising might be a good time to invade Northern Ireland, but plans never got off the ground.

**Eamon de Valera** excused his visit to the German Embassy in 1945, where he went to express his condolences at Hitler's death, by saying: 'I certainly was not going to add to his humiliation in the hour of defeat.'

### EMMET, ROBERT (1778–1803)

United Irishman who was born in Dublin and who met Napoleon in France. Though Napoleon was virtually surrounded by Irishmen – doctors, generals and aides – it was also a man born in Dublin, the **Duke of Wellington**, who defeated him at Waterloo. Wellington, the capital of New Zealand, is named after the Duke, while Emmet County, Iowa, is named after Emmet. Emmet was hanged, drawn and quartered in Thomas Street, Dublin, on 20 September 1803.

(See **Ogham**)

### EMPEROR'S WARRIORS

On 26 November 1985 an exhibition of part of the vast life-size collection of Chinese terracotta figures opened at the Royal Hospital, Kilmainham, Dublin. One of the figures, which date back to the 3rd century BC and are said to have guarded the tomb of China's first emperor against enemies both mortal and otherwise, received its first direct assault in over 2000 years when an electric light fitting fell on its head.

### ERIUGENA, JOHANNES SCOTUS (c. 810–77)

The philosophic face on the five pound note left his native Ireland in AD 847 to work for the West Frankish king, Charles the Bald, as the master of the palace school. Among other things, Eriugena denied the existence of hell, which may have been easy for someone who was going to spend so much time around money. Evelyn Waugh once remarked that to an Irishman there are only two fatal realities: Hell and the United States.

Johannes Scotus Eriugena was stabbed to death with pens by his students.

### EVOLUTION
The playwright J.M. Synge attributed his loss of religion to his reading of Darwin's *Origin of the Species* as a youth.

### EYEBROW
St Silan is said to have had such an impressive eyebrow that those who looked on it early in the morning immediately died. This led to the practice whereby potential suicides queued up at St Silan's door to catch a glimpse of the eyebrow when it was at its most dangerous.

### EYES
Arthur Jacob (1790–1874) was born in Portlaoise the same year as the Apostle of **Temperance**, Fr Theobald Mathew, but, instead of preaching against alcohol, he discovered a membrane of the eye since referred to as *Membrana Jacobi.* **Oscar Wilde**'s father, Sir William Wilde (1815–76), invented the Ophthalmoscope, an instrument for inspecting the interior of the retina. Before he went full-time as an actor and comedian in 1927, Jimmy O'Dea (1899–1965) worked in Dublin as an optician, having qualified in Scotland.

Bad eyesight and poverty at home are the reasons generally given for writer Sean O'Casey's leaving school at the age of nine.

St Derville is said to have gouged out her own eyes after being told they were her most attractive feature.

(See **Beauty**; **Burial**; **Horses**; **Marriage**; **Rats**)

## FAILURES

'A nation of brilliant failures, the Irish, who are too poetical to be poets' – Max Beerbohm, British author (1872–1956).

## FAIRY FORTS

Ancient mounds, often ringed with trees, believed by many to have been inhabited by fairies. One of the runways at Shannon's International Airport had originally been planned for a slightly different location, but had to be shifted because workmen refused to dig up a fairy fort in its proposed path.

Fairies themselves come in many guises. One creature to be immediately suspicious of is a white cow with red ears.

In 1678, the year that the poet Andrew Marvell died, a doctor from Wicklow by the name of Alan Moore was reported to have been abducted by fairies, though it is unlikely they were white cows with red ears.

## FAMINE

Though there have been many famines in Irish history, the great hunger which followed the failure of the potato crop due to blight in 1845 (caused by the fungus *Phytophtora infestans)* is the one which usually gets the capital letter. More than a million died of hunger in the period 1845–51 even though food was being exported through the ports. The Famine, or The Great Famine, was not something about which the world was unaware, and offers of assistance came from many sources, including a tribe of American Indians.

## FAT DAD
Acronym for the six counties of Ulster under British rule: Fermanagh, Antrim, Tyrone, Derry, Armagh, Down.

## FCA
Foras Cosanta Áitiúil (Local Defence Force). Often known as the Free Clothes Association. The FCA is the unarmed army reserve in the Republic.

## FENIANS
Founded in 1858, the Fenians were ambitious Irish rebels who, among other things, attempted to take over Canada. In June 1866 a group of some 800 armed men, under the command of Monaghan-born John O'Neill, crossed the Niagara River with the purpose of capturing the country of over 3.5 million square miles, intending to hold it to ransom in the cause of Irish freedom. However, on running out of supplies they were forced to retreat. A statement from Fenian headquarters followed: 'The Irish Republican Army has been in action for the first time.'

Sir Francis Hicks, who was Premier of Canada for three years and later Governor of Barbados, was born in Cork in 1807, though he was not a Fenian. Someone who was, however, was Stephen Meaney (1825–88) from Co. Clare, who somehow ended up writing the patriotic British song 'Three Cheers for the Red, White and Blue'.

**FIANNA**
Mythical warrior clan led by **Finn** (or Fionn)
**MacCumhaill**.

**FIANNA FÁIL**
'Soldiers of Destiny'. Mainstream, right of centre political party. A republican organization, it was formed by
those who had wanted to hold out for a 32-county
Ireland at the time of the **Treaty**.

**FIELD, JOHN (1782–1837)**
Dublin-born pianist and composer, and inventor of
the nocturne, who has a room in the National Concert
Hall named after him. Made a living for a time selling
the relatively new instrument, the piano. He lived in
Moscow (not the Irish one, see **Moscow**) and was a
teacher of Glinka, acknowledged as the father of modern Russian national music.

(See **Maternity**)

**FILTH**
The actress Jayne Mansfield's scheduled appearance
at the Mount Brandon Hotel in Tralee on 23 July
1967 was cancelled on moral grounds. Monsignor
Lane, PP, said: 'I appeal to the men and women, to the
boys and girls of Tralee, to dissociate themselves from
this attempt to besmirch the name of our town for the
sake of filthy gain.' Mansfield protested that she was
herself the mother of five children and a good
Catholic, but without success.

(See **Swift, Jonathan**; **Condom**)

**FINE GAEL**
Mainstream, right of centre political party. It was
formed by those who accepted the offer of 26 counties
at the time of the signing of the **Treaty**.

## FLANAGAN, OLIVER J. (1920–87)

Born in Mountmellick, Co. Laois, Oliver J. Flanagan was the longest-serving member of the Dáil, as well as one of the most 'colourful'. In 1943 he called for emergency orders 'directed against the Jews, who crucified our Saviour nineteen hundred years ago and who are crucifying us every day in the week... There is one thing that Germany did, and that was to rout the Jews out of their country. Until we rout the Jews out of this country, it does not matter what orders you make.' Some people, however, prefer to remember him as the naive young politician who went around with a 'Here comes Oliver' sign on his chest and another on his back saying 'There goes Oliver', or as the TD who in 1974 entered the Dáil bar for the first time for a book launch, though he had served in the house since 1943. In 1978 Flanagan received the Grand Order of St Gregory the Great from Pope John Paul II.

(See **Condom**)

## FLATULENCE

According to Dineley, it was a grave misdemeanour to break wind in 17th-century Ireland, the fart being 'so abominated by an Irishman that he either quarrels, or flees from you and crosseth himself'. Another authority, Fynes Moryson, tells of an Irish lord who banished 'his wife of a good family and beautiful, only for a fault as light as wind (which the Irish in general abhor)'. A report on flatulence by an anonymous writer of the 8th–12th century survives: '*Atá ben istír/Ní abraim a ainm/maidid essi a deilm/amal chloich a tailm.*' ('There's a woman in the land/her name I won't sing/but when she breaks wind/it's like a stone out of a sling.')

(See **Elizabeth I, Queen**)

## FLEAS

St Nannan may not be as well remembered as St Patrick, but he did once drive out an infestation of fleas from a village in Connaught. So well did he do the job in the unfortunately unnamed village that no flea has ever since returned.

(See **Ukelele**)

## FLIES

A morbid terror of flies drove eccentric genius, scientist and linguist Richard Kirwan (1733–1812) to place a reward on the head of each one splattered by his servants in his fashionable home in what is now Dublin's Parnell Square.

Flies were also very common pets for Irish saints. St Molong, we are told, had one, as did a number of others. St Mochua used his pet fly to mark the line and page of his hymnal when he fell asleep.

(See **Popes**)

## FOOT AND MOUTH

To prevent the notorious foot and mouth disease reaching Ireland, the number of people permitted to enter the country by sea and air was, on 7 December 1967, restricted to 2000 per day.

## FORGERY

Though William Henry Ireland (1777–1835) was an Englishman who had few connections with Ireland, he deserves mention here, not only because of his surname, but because of the similarity between what he did with the works of **Shakespeare** and what was done by the Irish Poet Laureate, Nahum Tate (1652–1715). Ireland, who was a famous, or infamous, forger of Shakespearian plays and manuscripts, finally worked up the courage to sign the Bard's name to a work wholly of his own hand. The 'discovery' of the lost manuscript would undoubtedly make him rich.

*Vortigern and Rowena*, however, despite the bard's moniker, was greeted with a deafening silence and Ireland was quickly exposed as the cheat that he was. However, in an ironic twist, and quick to turn the matter to his advantage, he went on to produce a successful book on his forging attempts, entitled *An Authentic Account of the Shakespearian MSS.*

### FORMORIANS

A mythical people who lived around Sligo and Donegal and on the island of Derinis and who, when trouble was brewing locally with the Nemedians, are said to have called on help from Greece to the tune of 60,000 soldiers by land and sea which led to 'the bloodiest battle of all time'.

### FORNICATION

The word comes from *fornix*, the Latin word for an arch. It was under the arches of the amphitheatres that prostitutes waited to satisfy the lust of important men after gladiatorial combat. In John Michelburne's play about the siege of Derry, written in 1705, Irish combatants are so cowardly they will prostitute their own families to save themselves:

> FRANC (an English Private): Shall I make Fornication upon thy Wife and Sister?
> IRISHMAN: Ay, Dau maake de Fornication upon my Wife, my Shister, and upon my Moder, and grand Moder, and shaave my life, Joy.

But it is not cowardice but love that prompts the same action in James Joyce's *Ulysses*: 'Greater love than this, he said, no man hath that a man lay down his wife for his friend.'

### FOXES

The traditional remedy for a thorn in one's foot was that the afflicted part should be rubbed with the tongue of a fox until the thorn came loose.

(See **Reincarnation**)

## FRANKENSTEIN

A novel by London-born Mary Shelley (1797–1851) which features Genovese scientist Victor Frankenstein, whose monstrous creation sets out to destroy his loved ones and ruin his life when he refuses to make a mate for it. One of the most devastating sections of the book, the murder by the monster of poor Victor's best friend, Clerval, takes place in an unnamed region of Ireland to which Victor has voyaged by boat, believing himself still to be in the Outer Hebrides.

(See **Beauty**)

## FRENCH, WILLIAM PERCY (1854–1920)

Clonquin, Co. Roscommon-born writer of many famous Irish songs, including 'Come Back, Paddy Reilly, to Ballyjamesduff' and 'Are ye right there, Michael?' Having started out working on a Board of Works drainage scheme in Co. Cavan, French became so popular abroad that he was able to tour the USA, Canada and the West Indies in 1888. But because he took out no copyright, he had no case when his songs were subsequently stolen by a London publisher.

## FRENCH REVOLUTION

One wonders what was so French about it. The storming of the Bastille on 14 July 1789 was led by an Irishman, James Blackwell (1763–1820), under the spiritual direction of an Irishman, the Abbé MacMahon, and the first prisoner released was an Irishman, Francis Xavier Whyte.

## FROGS

Chewing on frogs' legs, or indeed putting a live frog in your mouth, is considered to be a cure for toothache.

(See **Weather**)

## GAA

Gaelic Athletic Association. Founded in 1884 by Maurice Davin and Michael Cusack (1847–1906), the prototype for the Citizen in Joyce's *Ulysses*, the GAA enforces a ban on members of the British Armed Forces and Police from membership of the association. Its Rule 21 reads: 'A member of the association participating in dances or similar entertainment promoted by, or under the patronage of, such bodies, shall incur suspension of at least three months.' The first patron of the GAA was Archbishop Thomas Croke (1824–1902), a native of Mallow, Co. Cork, and after whom Croke Park stadium in Dublin is named.

## GAELTACHT

An area in Ireland where Irish is still spoken. The Gaeltacht Commission was set up in 1925 to study the few remaining Irish-speaking communities.

## GALWAY

West coast city. Christopher Columbus recorded a stop-over here in 1477 when he told of 'men of Cathay [who] have come towards the east. Of this we have seen many signs. And especially in Galway in Ireland, a man and a woman of extraordinary appearance, have come to land on two tree trunks.' According to some, what he probably saw were Eskimos washed off course in their kayak, but the account reminds one of the often forgotten maritime history of Ireland.

The term 'lynch mob' has its origins in Galway, too. In 1493, the year after Columbus 'discovered' America, the then chief magistrate of Galway, James Lynch Fitzstephen, found his own son, Walter, guilty of the murder of a Spanish visitor and had him executed. Some versions of the story even claim that, because the lad was so popular and no one would act as his hangman, the chief magistrate himself carried out the execution.

(See **Hy Brasil**)

## GANDHI, MOHANDÂS K. (1869–1948)
First called Mahatma ('Great Soul') by the Indian poet Rabindranath Tagore, Mohandâs K. Gandhi was one of the great spiritual figures of the 20th century. During his period of imprisonment for passive resistance, his special jailer was a Corkman by the name of Paddy Quinn. On one occasion Quinn, who had become a good friend of the Mahatma's, stopped a visitor in order to inspect the gift he was carrying. The gift turned out to be a biography of fellow Corkman and revolutionary **Michael Collins**.

## GARLIC
Helps to ward off **Dracula**, the creation of **Bram Stoker**. Political writer and commentator Conor Cruise O'Brien said of Charles J. Haughey in 1982: 'If I saw Mr Haughey buried at midnight at a crossroads, with a stake driven through his heart – politically speaking – I should continue to wear a clove of garlic round my neck, just in case.'

## GIVE IRELAND BACK TO THE IRISH
Title of a song recorded by Paul McCartney and Wings which topped the Irish charts for four weeks in February and March 1972.

## GLORIA
Country and Irish singing star whose 'One Day at a Time' was No.1 in the Irish charts for a total of 90 weeks in the late 1970s. Shortly afterwards the Irish record industry reviewed their methods for compiling charts.

## GOBSHITE
A fool, an idiot, a thick, a speaker of nonsensical or offensive diatribes. The word finally officially entered the English language in 1992, being included for the first time in Collins's *Concise English Dictionary*.

## GOD
The founder of the Church of God in the United States, John Walker, was born in Co. Roscommon in 1833.

The Ashanti people of Ghana, West Africa, have a sacred relic. It is the skull of Sir Charles McCarthy, a Corkman who was killed during a revolt in 1824.

## GOETHE, JOHANN WOLFGANG VON (1749–1832)
German poet, scholar and statesman who said: 'The Irish seem to me like a pack of hounds, always dragging down some noble stag.'

## GOGARTY, OLIVER ST JOHN (1878–1957)
Dublin-born surgeon, wit and writer who took and won a libel action against the poet **Patrick Kavanagh** for the following sentences which appeared in the latter's *The Green Fool*: 'I mistook Gogarty's white-robed maid for his wife – or his mistress. I expected every poet to have a spare wife.' During the Civil War of

1922–3, Gogarty almost drowned in the River Liffey where he had been attempting to escape a party of disgruntled Republicans. To commemorate his miraculous escape, Gogarty arranged to release two swans into the river. According to reports, however, the swans were reluctant to leave the box and Gogarty had to give it a kick to persuade them, surely relieving the moment of some of its poise.

## GOLD

The discovery of gold in the Wicklow hills in the 18th century started something of a gold rush. Though much of what was found was granular, one nugget weighed some 22 ounces. John William McKay, who was born in Dublin in 1831, discovered the Camstode Lode which started the great California Gold Rush of 1848, while another Irishman, Gabriel Read, discovered gold in New Zealand, giving rise to the gold rush there in 1861. Poor old **Charles Stewart Parnell**, however, tried to pan for enough of the precious metal near his home at Avondale, Co. Wicklow, to make Kitty O'Shea a ring for their wedding in June 1891, but just didn't have the gift.

Giraldus Cambrensis, the Welsh cleric and traveller, tells of the discovery at Carlingford in Ulster of a fish which had three gold teeth of some 50 ounces in weight. His claim that the sighting took place 'two years before the coming of the English' is however disputed by other accounts which say the sighting took place 400 years earlier and also claim that the fish was in fact a whale.

(See **Amputation**)

## GOLDSMITH, OLIVER (1728–74)

Novelist, poet, essayist and dramatist, who wrote, among other things, *The Deserted Village*, as well as essays, which included accounts from the life of **Carolan**. Failing to come to grips with his medical studies, Goldsmith took to travelling through Europe as a busker with his flute. Back in London, he began to write seriously, achieving almost instant success with his *The Vicar of Wakefield.* However when he produced a book on animals called *Animated Nature,* Dr Johnson pronounced: 'If he can tell a horse from a cow, that's as much as he knows about it.'

### GONNE, MAUD (MACBRIDE) (1866–1953)
Born in Aldershot, England on 19 December, the day after her parents' wedding, Maud Gonne was a strong-willed and independent woman. When the King of England visited Dublin, she flew a black petticoat on the end of a broom handle while everyone else waved their Union Jacks. She is, of course, equally famous as the object of **W.B. Yeats**'s passions. Though Yeats proposed to her almost on a yearly basis, it seems he was unable to persuade her at the time of the virtues of sexual intercourse, and it was Major John MacBride she finally married in 1903, converting to Catholicism to do so. Yeats later suggested she had ugly hands.

(See **Hair**)

### GOUT
Anne, Queen of Great Britain and Ireland (1665–1714), was suffering from gout when she had to be carried to her coronation on 23 April 1702, the day on which **Brian Boru** was killed in 1014 and on which both **William Shakespeare** and Miguel de Cervantes died in 1616.

### GPO
General Post Office. Located in the middle of Dublin's O'Connell Street, it was the scene of the 1916 Easter Rising around which Raymond Queneau's novel, *We Always Treat Women Too Well,* is set.

### GRATTAN, HENRY (1746–1820)
Dublin-born patriot, orator and MP who was in favour of Irish legislative independence. In May 1820, shortly before he died, Grattan travelled from Dublin to London, but was so ill he could not make the journey from Liverpool to London by coach and went by canal instead.

### GRAY, DORIAN
Fictional creation of **Oscar Wilde** who appears youthful and beautiful, while a hidden portrait shows the signs of age and excess.

### GREGORY, LADY AUGUSTA (1852–1932)
Playwright and one of the founders of the Abbey Theatre, Lady Gregory was the 12th of 16 children. It was at Coole Park where she lived, and where W.B. Yeats was a regular visitor that Lady Gregory, **AE**, **Jack** and **W.B. Yeats**, **George Bernard Shaw**, Augustus John and John Millington Synge carved their names on a tree in Ireland's most famous extant piece of graffiti. When she married William Gregory, a one-time Conservative MP for Dublin and Governor of Ceylon, Lady Gregory was a mature 28 years of age, while her husband was a mere 63.

### GROCERS
There were 12,681 of them in Ireland in 1967, the year Erin Foods Ltd. and H.J. Heinz Co. formed a joint company to market their groceries.

### GROUNDHOG
The North American marmot or woodchuck. Groundhog Day is the American name for Candlemas Day, 2 February. **James Joyce** was born on Groundhog Day in 1882. The writer James Stephens also claimed to have been born on 2 February 1882, but was more likely born on 9 February 1880.

## GUBU

Political catchword coined by Conor Cruise O'Brien in relation to Charles J. Haughey in August 1982: 'You've got to hand it to the man, you really have. He is grotesque, unbelievable, bizarre and unprecedented.' O'Brien's comment came after a series of bizarre events beginning with the murder of Nurse Bridie Gargan who had been sunbathing in the **Phoenix Park**, Dublin, in July of that year. After beating her unconscious, her assailant, Malcolm MacArthur, took the nurse's car with her inside to make his escape and was, at one stage, spotted by the driver of an ambulance who, unwittingly, cleared the escape route for what he thought was an accident victim. MacArthur followed the ambulance to St James Hospital and then made off at speed. Two days later he turned up in Edenderry, Co. Offaly, answering a newspaper advertisement about a gun for sale. MacArthur took the gun from the young farmer, Donal Dunne, who had offered it for sale, and shot him through the head with it. When it was found that MacArthur had been staying in the home of the Attorney General, Patrick Connolly, who was oblivious to the fact that his house guest was Ireland's most wanted man, the plot really thickened, resulting in Connolly's resignation and pressure for the resignation of the then Taoiseach, Charles Haughey.

At another time during the extensive manhunt for MacArthur, the fugitive was in the VIP box in Croke Park, attending the All-Ireland Hurling semi-final.

MacArthur was finally captured and convicted of the murder of Nurse Gargan, but the charges relating to the murder of Donal Dunne were not pursued. John Banville's novel *The Book of Evidence* recounts a remarkably similar story to that of the MacArthur case and is believed to be closely modelled on same.

## GUEVARA, ERNESTO 'CHÉ' (1928–67)

Bolivian radical reputedly descended from the Lynchs of Clare, which is unlikely to be the reason his familiar name suggests the Irish 'Shay' or 'Seamus'. It should be remembered that a number of Irish coffin ships arrived in Guevara's general area of the world in the middle of the last century. Michael D. Higgins and others have traced the remains of an Irish-speaking community as far as Montserrat in the West Indies.

When one John Perrot (or Perot), a travelling Quaker preacher, was imprisoned in Kilkenny for annoying the city authorities, he met 120 of these emigrants who were being sent to Barbados. Perrot, however, was released and on 6 June 1658, undeterred, went to Rome where, filled with religious zeal, he attempted to convert Pope Alexander VII (no relation to Alexander Pope, the English poet who said Ireland was 'the mother of sweet singers'). For this affrontery, Perrot was again imprisoned and this time tortured. In 1662, at last released from Rome, and in the meantime having been imprisoned in Ireland and Newgate, he accepted voluntary deportation for his 'crimes' – to Barbados.

## GUINNESS, ARTHUR (1725–1803)

Kildare-born founder of the famous brewery in 1759 and the father of 21 children, Guinness founded the first Sunday School in Ireland in 1786. In the early days the stout was known as 'Guinness's black Protestant porter' because of Arthur's opposition to the United Irishmen. Later Dublin Corporation tried to disconnect his water supply and Arthur threatened the officials with a pickaxe. The Guinness family remained in control of the brewery until Lord Iveagh was succeeded by Ernest Saunders (dubbed 'Deadly Ernest'), the first chairman who was not a Guinness, and who was subsequently convicted of fraud during the bid to take over the Distillers' Group.

## GULLIVER'S TRAVELS

Fantastical novel by **Jonathan Swift**, featuring the eponymous hero in his adventures with Lilliputians and Yahoos.

## HAIR

When the playwright Sean O'Casey remarked of **Maud Gonne** that she had 'long lovely yellow hair' it is hard to say whether he was alluding to the fact that long, loose hair on a woman in the 15th to 17th centuries had been a sign that the wearer was single, while hair bound up at the back of the head signified marriage.

## HAMILTON, SIR WILLIAM ROWAN (1805–65)

Mathematician, poet and astronomer, born in Dublin, who spent his life working in Dunsink Observatory. A child prodigy, Hamilton educated himself in mathematics and 13 languages other than his native English (Arabic, French, German, Greek, Hebrew, Hindustani, Italian, Latin, Malay, Persian, Sanskrit, Spanish and Syriac). At 17 he discovered a mathematical error in Laplace's monumental five-volume work, *Celestial Mechanics*, and at 22 was appointed Professor of Astronomy at **Trinity College** Dublin, as well as Astronomer Royal of Ireland. He was knighted at the age of 30. Discovered that in calculating for three dimensions, the commutative law of multiplication does not necessarily hold. Spent the remainder of his life drinking heavily.

## HAMLET
A tragedy by **William Shakespeare** in which the eponymous protagonist is heard to swear by **St Patrick.** The original Hamlet on whom the play is based was actually killed by an Irish king. Shakespeare's other great tragedy, *Macbeth*, concerns a real king who was of Irish descent.

## HANDBALL
Popular pursuit among Christian Brothers.

## HANDEL, GEORGE FRIEDERIC (1685–1759)
German-born composer who arrived in Ireland in 1741 and whose *Messiah* was first performed in Fishamble Street, Dublin, on 13 April 1742. According to Beethoven, 'He was the greatest composer that ever lived,' though when Sir Isaac Newton heard him play, according to Joseph Warton, he could 'find nothing to remark but the elasticity of his fingers'.

## HANGING
Method of execution of, especially, witches, patriots and other subversives. Males are said to ejaculate at the point of death and the plant *Belladonna*, or deadly nightshade, is said to grow only on soil on which the dead man's semen falls.

Of the many unusual accounts of hangings, that of a 19th-century criminal named Gallagher, near Pontoon in Co. Mayo, commands attention. Having stolen the horse of the magistrate who came to arrest him, and then returning it with a note congratulating the magistrate on his choice of mount, Gallagher was finally arrested and brought to the scaffold, together with a sidekick by the name of Walsh. Though Walsh died, Gallagher's rope broke and, while a second noose was being prepared, Gallagher was seen to drink a glass of wine and chat amiably with the expectant crowd. The second noose, however, bore the strain.

(See **Reincarnation**)

## HARP

The harp is the national symbol of Ireland.

Something that may surprise many is the fact that it was Henry VIII who first introduced the harp on Irish coins. The first issue of groats and half-groats in his time carried the initials of three of his queens, 'K' for Katherine of Aragon, 'A' for Anne Boleyn (who was born in Ireland) and 'I' for Jane Seymour. Perhaps another explanation for the 'heads' and 'tails' confusion.

(See **Churchill**; **Contradiction**)

## HASCUFF

Dublin-based Viking leader executed by Strongbow's Normans after their arrival in 1169. Strongbow is also said to have cut his own son in two because the boy was cowardly.

## HAW HAW, LORD (1906–46)

Real name William Joyce. Born in New York, Joyce moved to Galway where he attended school and then to London, and finally to Germany. Hanged in Britain on 3 January 1946 after being found guilty of treason for his propagandist broadcasts on Radio Hamburg in support of the Axis forces during World War II. After the war he had escaped to Denmark *en route* to Sweden, but his famous voice was recognized and he was apprehended while also being shot in the thigh. Had Joyce not earlier forged papers which claimed he was a British subject, as a non-national he could not have been tried and executed for treason. His remains were removed to Bohermore cemetery in Galway in 1976.

## HEAD
Affectionate term for Dubliners, as in the greeting, 'How's it going, head?'

(See **Carolan, Turlough**; **Cromwell, Oliver**)

## HEANEY, SEAMUS (b. 1939)
Derry-born poet, critic and playwright who was Professor of Poetry at Oxford and Bolyston Professor of Rhetoric at Harvard. Known widely and affectionately as 'Famous Seamus'.

(See **UFO**)

## HEIGHT
The Irish Fairy, Katherine Kelly, who died in childbirth in Norfolk, England in 1735, was a mere 34 inches tall and weighed just 28 pounds.

The most famous Irish giant was Patrick Cotter O'Brien who was born near Kinsale in 1760 where he was sold by his father for £50 to a travelling circus. O'Brien, who claimed he was 9 foot tall, was found to be, in fact, 7 foot 11 inches when he died in 1801. This is considerably shorter than the tallest American, Robert Wadlow, who measured 8 foot 11 inches. Nevertheless O'Brien is the tallest Irishman for whom official records exist.

An Irishman who was 7 foot at the age of 16 was Cornelius Magrath who died in 1759.

In 1895 the *Strand* magazine reported that a fossilized Irish giant had been discovered in the Broad

Street Depot of the London and North Western Railway. It was the property of a showman named Dyer or Dwyer, who claimed he had found it while prospecting for iron in the hills of Antrim. The fossil weighed almost two tons and was more than 12 feet tall. The right foot had six toes.

(See **Berkeley, George**)

### HERZOG, CHAIM
Israeli President who was born in Belfast in 1918.

### HITCHCOCK, ALFRED (1899–1980)
The thriller/chiller producer/director was born in London to an Irish mother, Emma Whelan from Cork.

### HONE, NATHANIEL (1718–84)
The Elder. Dublin-born painter, famous for his portraits from the English provinces and for his imputations of plagiarism on the part of Sir Joshua Reynolds. The other Nathaniel Hone was Nathaniel Hone II (1831–1917) who was a landscape painter, fond of pastoral and coastal scenes, and who spent much of his time in France. A non-Nathaniel Hone was Evie, who worked primarily in stained glass and was among the first artists in Ireland who could be considered abstract.

### HONORARY CITIZENS
Irish international soccer squad manager, Jack Charlton, is one of only six people to have been made honorary citizens of Ireland. The others are Chester Beatty (whose collection of ancient manuscripts left to the state includes the world's oldest copy of the New Testament), Dutch industrialist Tiede Herrema (who was at the centre of a kidnapping siege at Monasterevin) and his wife Elisabeth, and Tip O'Neill (Speaker of the US House of Representatives) and his wife Mildred.

## HOPKINS, GERARD MANLEY (1844–89)

Jesuit poet. The youngest of nine children in a High
Anglican family, Hopkins converted to Catholicism in
1866, entered the Jesuits in 1868 and was ordained a
priest nine years later. From 1884 until his death he
was Professor of Classics at University College Dublin.

## HORSES

It was in Wellington Barracks in the Co. Tipperary
town of Cahir that a horse known as 'Crimea Bob' was
buried in 1862 with full military honours. Bob had
served the 11th Hussars in the Crimea and took part
in the famous Charge of the Light Brigade at
Balaklava from which the hood or stocking with cut-
out eyes and nose worn by paramilitaries gets its
name.

Another Irish horse of distinction was Captain
Myles Keogh's mount, Comanche, who, in 1876, was
the only survivor of Custer's last stand. When
Comanche finally died his innards were removed and
ceremoniously buried while his outsides were stuffed
by one Professor Lewis Cyche and are now exhibited
at the University of Kansas Museum of Natural
History, Lawrence.

The *Irish Independent* of 20 January 1994 reported
the growing concern of horse breeders near a village
in Co. Kildare after reports that the Dun Laoghaire-
Rathdown County Council was appealing a decision to
refuse them permission to open a massive rubbish
dump in the area. The Council maintained that their
project would not create 'the health, litter, traffic,
visual and environmental problems which had been
claimed'. The name of the village where the dump was
to be sited was Kill.

When the IRA kidnapped Shergar, the fourth Aga
Khan's prize-winning racehorse, from Ballymany
Stables on 8 February 1983, they may not have been
aware they had chosen the feast day of St John of

Matha for their crime. The saint is best remembered for his efforts to ransom prisoners from their Moslem enemies.

## HURLING
Fastest grass-based game in the world. A hurling team consists of 13 men armed with sticks fashioned from specially grown ash – most of which is now imported from Wales – used to propel a *sliothar*, an orange-sized ball. About the year 1755 the Irish in London held regular hurling matches to the rear of the British Museum.

(See **CúChulainn**)

## HURT, JOHN
English movie-star of *The Elephant Man*, *The Field* and *1984*. Now living in Ballintubbert in the house where the Poet Laureate Cecil Day-Lewis was born in 1904.

## HY BRASIL
Imaginary island 30 miles off the coast of Galway, which nevertheless featured on maps right up to the 16th century.

## HYDE, DOUGLAS (1860–1949)
Born in Sligo, on the same day as Anton Chekhov, Hyde left school at the age of 13. He wrote in Irish under the pen name *An Craoibhin Aoibhinn* ('The Delightful Little Branch') and became first President of the Republic of Ireland in 1938. He also wrote what is considered the first modern play in the Irish language, *Casadh an tSúgáin*, and *A Literary History of Ireland*. Co-founder of the Gaelic League.

(See **RTE**)

## ICE

An iceberg was responsible for the deaths of 1513 people on 14 April 1912, when the White Star liner *Titanic* collided with one near Newfoundland and sank on its maiden voyage. Among those killed was the *Titanic*'s designer, Thomas Andrews. *Olympic*, the little known sister ship of *Titanic*, was more fortunate. Instead of hitting an iceberg it hit a German U-boat, on purpose, and survived while the submarine sank.

According to Charles Fort, chronicler of the strange and bizarre, there is evidence that a 1 kg block of ice fell from the sky in Cashel in June 1974.

Eugene O'Neill, America's greatest 20th-century playwright and author of *The Iceman Cometh*, was the son of Kilkenny-born actor, James O'Neill.

## ICELAND

Discovered by the Irish in AD 795. Fishermen from the two countries regularly visit each other's waters, usually in a clandestine manner.

## INDUSTRY
'No nation in Europe is less given to industry or is more phlegmatic than this' – Giovanna Battista Rinuccini (1592–1653), Papal Nuncio to the Irish Confederate Catholics, speaking about the Irish.

## INSTRUCTION
The Athlone-born tenor, Count John McCormack (1884–1945), beat the young **James Joyce** in a singing competition in 1904, which may have been a useful lesson for Joyce, prompting him to stick to writing. But if Joyce was not destined to be a tenor, he was at least destined to be the tenner (£10) in the series of new notes designed by Robert Ballagh.

A useful lesson in the operation of the sextant, a device necessary for navigation and exploration, was given by the Tyrone-born astronomer Thomas Maclear (1794–1879) to Dr David Livingstone, the Scottish missionary and explorer of Africa. Incidentally, according to Livingstone, one of the tribal greetings he came across on his travels was 'What do you dance?' because each tribe had its own distinctive steps.

## INVASIONS
(For the Irish invasion of Canada, see **Fenians**. For the Irish invasion of England, see **Pretender**.)

## IRA
Irish Republican Army. Declared an illegal organization in the Republic of Ireland in 1936.

(See **Aircraft; Zenda, The Prisoner of**)

## IRELAND, THE GREAT BOOK OF
Single-volume, one-off manuscript from the hands of 140 poets (including **Samuel Beckett**, **Seamus Heaney** and Ted Hughes), 120 painters (including Louis Le Brocquy and Sir Sidney Nolan), 9 composers and 2 calligraphers. A latter-day **Book of Kells** with

an asking price of £1.3 million, it has yet to find a home. A newspaper cartoon at the time of its unveiling posited the notion that buyers would have to wait for the paperback edition.

## IRELAND, REPUBLIC OF
The first announcement that Ireland had become a republic was made by the then Taoiseach, John A. Costello, on 7 September 1948 – in Ottawa, Canada.

## IRELAND, WILLIAM HENRY (1777–1835)
(See **Forgery**)

## IRISH
Of Ireland. Most dictionaries agree on this. Where they begin to disagree is on the secondary meaning. The *Penguin English Dictionary*, updated in 1992, suggests 'amusingly illogical', while the entry in the *Collins Concise Dictionary* of 1990 goes somewhat further with 'offensive, ludicrous or illogical'. The *Concise Oxford Dictionary* of 1984 lists the secondary meaning as 'resembling the Irish, esp. w. ref. to their reputation for illogicality'. So, illogicality agreed, all that remains to be settled is the degree of same.

An interesting departure from the usual deliberations about what 'Irish' might mean is to be found in the *Dictionary of American Slang*, edited by Robert L. Chapman and published by Pan. Though it does not get involved in the illogicality debate, it does offer a rare morsel under the phrase 'The Irish Way', which it cites as 'heterosexual anal penetration', going on to explain that the term was the result of experimentation among the Irish to avoid pregnancy.

## IRISH COFFEE
Invented by Dublin-born chef Joe Sheridan while working in Foynes, Co. Limerick, in 1943. A plaque for this earth-shattering invention was unveiled at

Shannon Airport on 15 November 1975.

### IRISH WOMEN
Those women with the shortest lifespan in the EC.

Iris Murdoch (b. 1919), the Dublin-born novelist, who was the first Irish person to win the Booker Prize with her novel *The Sea, The Sea* in 1978, once said: 'I think being a woman is like being Irish... Everyone says you're important and nice but you take second place all the same.'

Certainly, there was not much until recently to indicate that the general view of Irish women had changed significantly since US President 'Teddy' Roosevelt said in 1907 that, 'beauty, soft voice, sweet speech, wisdom, needlework and chastity' were the attributes of the perfect Irish woman.

And, on the subject of chastity, when Welshman Edward Lhuyd travelled around the country in 1700, he found that Irish women used the wild flower St Dabeoc's Heath to protect their chastity, though he neglected to explain how.

(See **Ankles**)

There is no J in the Irish alphabet.

### JACONIUS

Jaconius was the name of the whale on which **St Brendan**, 'the Navigator', stopped and inadvertently lit a fire, mistaking it for a small island.

On 13 March 1983 a 63-foot whale was washed up on the shore at Bunmahon in Co. Waterford.

### JAM

Kent-born Sir Tyrone Guthrie (1900–71), the theatre producer, who left his house at Annaghmakerrig in Co. Monaghan to the state so that it might be used as a retreat for writers and artists, helped to start a jam and preserves factory in nearby Newbliss, but the project failed in the year of his death.

### JAMES, JESSE (1847–81)

American outlaw whose ancestors came from Asdee in Co. Kerry, where mass continued to be said for him until 1959 by a priest called Fr Ferris. James's grandfather came from Asdee and Jesse was born in Montana during the Great Famine. In Hollywood mythology James dies after being shot in the back while affixing a picture of the Virgin Mary to his cabin wall.

## JFK

(See **Kennedy, John Fitzgerald**)

## JOHN PAUL II, POPE (b. 1920)

Formerly Karol Wojtyla, playwright, singer, poet and goalkeeper. As well as being Pope, he is the Bishop of Kilfenora, Co. Clare, a tiny diocese which failed to join any of its neighbours due to ancient tribal disputes, and so falls under the direct authority of Rome.

## JOHNSON, SAMUEL (1709–84)

English poet, critic and lexicographer: 'The Irish are a fair people; They never speak well of one another.'

## JOYCE, JAMES (1882–1941)

Author. The oldest of 15 children, only 10 of whom survived infancy, Joyce is credited with being the originator of the modern novel. His most famous work, *Ulysses*, was inspired by Homer. Joyce's other great work, *Finnegans Wake*, ends with the word 'The'. He was the manager of Ireland's first cinema, the Volta, in Dublin's Mary Street in 1909–10 and took Irish lessons from the patriot **Patrick Pearse**. He is buried in Fluntern cemetery in Zurich, close to the Zoo.

(See **Groundhog**)

## JUDGES

An Irish judge who once sentenced 97 men to their deaths in one day was the infamous Lord Norbury whose eccentric and unpredictable courtrooms attracted much attention. He even allowed the presence of a drunk at his side who shouted from time to time 'Find for the plaintiff' to the great amusement of the onlookers. **Daniel O'Connell** was among those who made efforts to have Norbury removed, but without success.

A judge who possibly spent much of the rest of his life in prayer was the one who tried Doctor Pierce Creagh in Cork in 1705. False witnesses having been arranged to put the good doctor away on a trumped-up charge, the judge sat in shock as the floor of the courtroom collapsed, taking the whole assembly with it and killing one of the 'witnesses' outright. Creagh, miraculously, stayed in place and was unharmed. The judge acquitted him.

The first woman judge to be appointed to the High Court was Mella Carroll from Dublin, on 3 October 1980.

There is no K in the Irish alphabet.

## KAISER
Title of German rulers, the most famous of whom was Kaiser Wilhelm II: 'I would have liked to go to Ireland, but my grandmother [Queen Victoria] would not let me. Perhaps she thought I wanted to take the little place.'

## KAVANAGH, PATRICK (1905–67)
Monaghan-born poet and novelist who went to live in Dublin in 1939. Among his most famous works are *The Green Fool, Tarry Flynn* and *The Great Hunger*. Six months before his death on 30 November (67 years to the day after **Oscar Wilde**) Kavanagh married his long-time friend Katherine Moloney, but following her death a bizarre wrangle started as to whether Kavanagh had ever consummated the marriage and whether his estate should have fallen to his wife or to his brother, Peter. Peter Kavanagh's biography of his poet brother, *Sacred Keeper*, makes no mention of Katherine, though she and Patrick lived together on and off in London for some ten years before getting

married. There is even a photograph in the book, taken after their wedding, from which Katherine has been removed. The most recent development in the dispute was the removal by Peter of a gravestone from over the poet's remains in Inniskeen, where Katherine is also buried, back to the Kavanagh family homestead at nearby Mucker.

(See **Nobel Prize**)

### KELLS, BOOK OF
The most famous of the Irish monastic vellum manuscripts, now housed in Trinity College Dublin, the 9th-century Book of Kells draws visitors from around the world and is to many a symbol of Irish literary, artistic and religious tradition. Consisting of 340 leaves measuring approximately 13 by 9 inches, the Book of Kells was, it is believed, for the most part made on Iona off the coast of Scotland.

### KENNEDY, JOHN FITZGERALD (1917–63)
Irish-American President of the United States, assassinated in Dallas on 22 November 1963. The word 'assassin' has the same root as the word 'hashish' and was originally applied in Persia and Syria to bodyguards who used the drug. Though a campaigner for human rights and liberty, Kennedy has also been the subject of countless allegations over his use of drugs and his connections with the actress Marilyn Monroe.

Whether or not he was fond of narcotics, JFK did have a weakness for cigars. According to his former press secretary, Pierre Salinger, Kennedy sent out for a thousand of his favourite brand, Petit Upmann, the day before he imposed a ban on the import of cigars from Cuba.

Someone who evidently shared Kennedy's love of smoking was **Oscar Wilde** who said tobacco was 'the perfect pleasure' because 'it always leaves one unsatisfied'.

In 1963 there were no health warnings on cigarette packets in Ireland. Neither was it a federal felony to kill a president of the United States.

(See **Bees**)

### KERRY BLUE
A breed of dog believed to have been brought to Ireland by the survivors of the Spanish Armada washed ashore on the south western coasts. The coastline of Ireland, incidentally, is officially estimated at 5800 km.

### KIERKEGAARD, SØREN (1813–55)
Danish philosopher and theologian who believed the Irish male to be baptized with one arm out of the water 'so that in after life he can grasp a sword and hold a girl in his arm'.

### KILKENNY
Midland city of Norman origin. The infamous Statutes of Kilkenny, passed in 1367, forbade amongst other things the intermarriage of Irish and English and the wearing of Irish clothes by English settlers. Among the items of clothing peculiar to Ireland are the **báinín**, the *crios* or woollen belt, **brogues** and pairs of *mairtíní*. These latter were footless stockings. It is traditionally considered unwise to kill a cricket because its relatives will come and make holes in your stockings.

### KODAK
Camera and film manufacturing company which built a factory in the shape of a slide projector in the midland town of Newbridge.

## LATE LATE SHOW, THE
Cult TV show hosted by Gay Byrne (b. 1934) on which the audience sing or recite poems to their loved ones at home and the guests talk to each other about their latest books on dieting.

## LAUGHTER
Anthony Trollope, the English writer of the Barchester novels, who came to Ireland at the age of 26 and was stationed at Banagher, Co. Offaly, where he worked as a Post Office Surveyor, is credited with reforming the Irish postal system. Described by Henry James as 'the dullest Briton of them all', ironically Trollope literally died laughing when he suffered a stroke during the reading by his niece of F. Antsey's comic novel *Vice Versa*.

## LAWRENCE, D[AVID] H[ERBERT] (1885–1930)
English novelist, poet and painter who said in a 1927 letter: 'Ireland is to my mind something like the bottom of an aquarium, with little people in crannies like prawns.'

## LENIN

Sean MacBride (1904–88), the patriot and international statesman who was born in Paris, was the only Irish recipient of the Nobel and Lenin Peace Prizes, as well as the American Medal of Justice.

## LEPRECHAUNS

It is thought that the notion of the existence of these little creatures originates with the stories of the Tuatha de Danann, a magic-practising tribe who worshipped the goddess Dana, and who were driven into subterranean hiding by the Milesians.

(See **Marvell, Andrew**)

## LIA FÁIL

The Lia Fáil was the Stone of Destiny which once graced the hill of Tara and on which the High Kings of Ireland were crowned. It was lent to Scotland in the 6th century for the coronation of the High King's brother Fergus, but was never returned. In 1297, it was 'borrowed' from Scotland and taken by Edward I to Westminster Abbey, where it remains to this day. In 1950, a Scottish Nationalist Group briefly repossessed it after forcibly entering Westminster and attempting to take it back up north.

## LIBRARIES

Narcissus Marsh (1638–1713) was Anglican Archbishop of, in succession, Cashel (1691), Dublin (1694) and Armagh (1703), but was also a bibliophile who found time to found the country's first public library, in Dublin, which is named for him.

A library that was captured at sea and sold in Salem, Massachusetts, was that of Richard Kirwan (1733–1812), President of the Royal Irish Academy. The library, which was *en route* from Galway to London, was taken by a privateer captain and removed to America for sale.

## LIMERICK

South-western city and county. Limerick is also the name of a five-line verse form popularized by Edward Lear and others, and reputedly invented by a Limerick publican as a form of amusement for his customers.

(See **Irish Coffee; Bollix**)

## LISDOONVARNA

A small Co. Clare spa town which fills with bachelors for its yearly festival, Lisdoonvarna was once the venue for a major yearly rock and folk festival. One of the few people with Clare connections not mentioned in Christy Moore's song of the same name is Muhammad Ali, three times World Heavyweight Champion, whose maternal grandfather was an O'Grady from that county.

### LISZT, FRANZ (1811–86)

Hungarian composer and pianist who toured Ireland and England in 1840–41 and of whom the English *Dramatic and Musical Review* of 1843 said, 'He writes the ugliest music extant.' Liszt must have felt like getting back to Ireland and out of the way. But if you think he could have cheered himself up with some delicacies from the Hungarian-Jewish pork butcher, Dlugacz, whom Joyce was to mention a generation later in *Ulysses* as being located on Dublin's Dorset Street, you would be wrong. Dlugacz never existed. The shop is one of the few inventions in the meticulously researched streetscapes of Joyce's masterpiece.

The gridwork of Dublin's streetscape was designed by Humphrey Jervis who became Lord Mayor of the city in 1681.

## LIVER

The liver of Irishwoman Mary Kelly, who was the last victim of the infamous Jack the Ripper, was torn out and left between the legs of the corpse. Liver, along with 'thick giblet soup, nutty gizards' and 'a stuffed roast heart', was a favourite food of Leopold Bloom, hero of Joyce's *Ulysses*. Ireland's first human liver transplant was carried out in St Vincent's Hospital, Dublin, on 19 April 1985.

(See **Aphrodisiac**)

## LOGAN, JOHNNY

Real name Seán Sherrard, Logan was the only person to watch himself win the Eurovision Song Contest on more than one occasion. In 1992 he wrote but did not perform the winning song. However, his first win with Shay Healy's 'What's Another Year?', though it lasted two weeks in the UK charts, left again quicker than any other UK No.1.

## LONG FELLOW, THE

(See **de Valera, Eamon**)

## LOVE

'In Ireland there is so little sense of compromise that a girl has to choose between perpetual adoration and perpetual pregnancy' – George Moore.

When Katharine 'Kitty' O'Shea (1845–1921) began an affair with the patriot and Home Rule activist **Charles Stewart Parnell**, she could not have imagined how badly it would end for both of them. Inevitably, her husband, Captain O'Shea, discovered the goings-on and decided to expose them by pressing charges. Kitty, and particularly her political lover, were disgraced in the most famous divorce scandal in Irish history.

But this was not to put the lovers off. Having had three children by him between 1882 and 1884, Kitty finally agreed to marry Parnell, which she did in 1891. However, he died in her arms a mere 14 weeks later. Katharine survived him by 30 years.

## LUGHANASA

Pagan festival in the month of August, named after the god Lugh, as is the French town of Lyons.

Brian Friel's play *Dancing at Lughanasa* was an enormous success on Broadway in 1992.

## LYNOTT, PHIL (1951–85)

Self-proclaimed 'Black Irish Bastard' and front man with Thin Lizzy, the band named after a character in *The Beano,* who brought Ireland to the international rock music world. Lynott died as a result of heroin addiction. The video for his single 'Old Town' is widely considered the first Irish classic.

(See **Stamps**)

## MACBRIDE, MAUD
(See **Gonne, Maud**)

## MACCUMHAILL, FINN
Leader of the mythical warrior clan, the Fianna. Finn or Fionn is also behind the legend of the origins of the Giant's Causeway in Co. Antrim. According to the story, it was he who tore up the causeway which originally went all the way to Scotland, because he feared a giant called Finn Gall would use it to cross the water and defeat him. The present unique basalt rock formation is said to be the remains of the original land-connection and is composed of some 37,000 columns.

## MCGOWRAN, JACK (1918–73)
Dublin-born actor best known for his performances in the plays of Samuel Beckett. McGowran was the first non-American to win the New York Critics' 'Actor of the Year' Award, in 1971. He died in New York during a performance of Sean O'Casey's *The Plough and the Stars*.

## MADNESS
'For the great Gaels of Ireland/Are the men that God made mad,/For all their wars are merry,/And all their

songs are sad.' So wrote G.K. Chesterton in 'The Ballad of the White Horse' (1911). In fact, the madness of the Irish has much been commented upon. 'Now Ireland has her madness and her weather still,' wrote Auden in his 'In Memory of W.B. Yeats'.

In 1984 there were nearly 12,000 patients in the Republic's psychiatric hospitals, representing 0.4% of the population.

## MALACHY, SAINT (c. 1094–1148)
The founder of Mellifont Abbey in 1142, the first Cistercian Abbey in Ireland, Malachy became Archbishop of Armagh, and died at Clairvaux *en route* to Rome in St Bernard's arms, leaving Bernard to write his life story which he imaginatively entitled *The Life of St Malachy of Armagh*. The so-called Prophecies of St Malachy were unknown before 1590.

St Malachy's feast day, 3 November, is the birthday of the Taoiseach, Albert Reynolds.

## MALNUTRITION
James Clarence Mangan (1803–49), the Dublin-born author of 'Dark Rosaleen' and the subject of Louis D'Alton's play *The Man in the Cloak* was born in Fishamble Street where **Handel**'s *Messiah* had first been performed 61 years earlier. A noted translator of the German romantic poets, Mangan died of malnutrition in Dublin's Meath Hospital.

## MALONE, MOLLY
Dublin vendor of cockles and mussels who was more than likely a prostitute. Malone's death of a fever probably resulted from over-exposure to the chest if the statue of her on Dublin's Lower Grafton Street can be believed.

The notion of farming mussels, a kind of edible bivalve mollusc found in the sea, is attributed to an Irishman by the name of Walton. When shipwrecked near La Rochelle in 1235, Walton set out to trap birds along the seashore in a net attached to poles. When the tide went out he found the only things he had managed to catch with his invention were mussels.

## MANIA

Theatre mania was certainly experienced by Joseph Holloway (1861–1944) of Dublin, who attended every theatrical performance of whatever merit he could physically manage to get to and, in the process, wrote some 25 million words in the 221 volumes that make up his journals in the National Library of Ireland, excerpts of which were published in 1967 in a single volume entitled *James Holloway's Abbey Theatre.*

## MARCONI

The headquarters of RTE is situated in the grounds of what used to be Montrose House, once owned by the Jameson family, famous for their whiskey. Marrying an Italian, Anne Jameson, who had grown up in Montrose, had a son in Bologna on 25 April 1884. The son was Guglielmo Marconi and it was he who was responsible for the wireless telegraphy which makes RTE transmissions possible.

As well as having an Irish mother, Marconi also had an Irish wife, Beatrice O'Brien, whom he married in 1905.

## MARKIEVICZ, COUNTESS CONSTANCE, née Gore-Booth (1868–1927)

London-born revolutionary and author of *A Call to the Women of Ireland*, Markievicz became an officer in the Irish Citizen Army, causing Sean O'Casey to resign. She was given the death sentence because of her involvement in the 1916 Easter Rising, but her sentence was commuted on account of her sex. Such kid-glove treatment was hardly appropriate for a woman who was independent and courageous enough to go on hunger strike for a time in 1923. She was also the first woman elected to the House of Commons, but did not take up her seat.

## MARRIAGE

The average Irish bridegroom is 27.4 years of age, while the average bride is 25.3. In 1200 Pope Innocent III wrote to the Archbishop of Lunden to complain that polygamy was rampant in Ireland and that there were then no marriage ceremonies to speak of. In 1634 it was even necessary to pass a law in the Irish parliament to enforce monogamy.

*Brewer's Dictionary of Phrase and Fable*, 3rd edition, informs us: 'When a person has a black eye we sometimes say to him, "You have been to an Irish wedding, I see," because the Irish are more famous for giving their guests on these occasions *black eyes* than *white favours*.'

## MARTYRS

On 27 September 1992, the Catholic Church beatified seventeen 16th-century Irish martyrs, among them three sailors, a baker, a Jesuit brother, seven priests from various orders, three bishops and an archbishop. All had been executed for failing to renounce their religion by taking the Oath of Supremacy.

But the seventeenth and most horrific execution was that of the only woman among the number selected and approved by Rome. Co. Meath woman Margaret Ball (neé Birmingham) (c. 1515–84) had provided 'safe houses' for priests and clerics on the run. But when her son Walter converted to Protestantism and subsequently became the Mayor of Dublin, he saw to it that his errant mother was arrested, drawn through the streets on a wooden frame and imprisoned in Dublin Castle, where she died sometime in the late 1580s.

## MARVELL, ANDREW (1621–78)

One of the most famous poems of the English poet Andrew Marvell, 'An Horation Ode upon Cromwell's Return from Ireland', recounts the Lord Protector's adventures in quelling the natives in Ireland: 'And now the Irish are ashamed/To see themselves in one year tamed.' Marvell was secretary for a time to the poet John Milton who was in turn for a time secretary to Cromwell.

(See **Fairy Forts**)

## MATERNITY

The first public maternity hospital in these islands was the Rotunda, founded in 1745 by Laoisman Bartholomew Mosse (1712–59). The first patient, one Judith Rochford, was admitted on 15 March 1745. In the first years the death rate among new-born babies was as high as one in six. The Rotunda itself was designed by the German architect, Richard Cassels, and it was here that the pianist **John Field** (1782–1837) gave his first public recital at the age of nine.

## MERCENARIES

Irish mercenaries have fought in many wars around the world, but few have earned themselves the disgrace which was heaped upon a group who went to Venezuela to aid the struggle of Simon Bolivar (1783–1830), the Liberator of Latin America who, incidentally, was in correspondence with Ireland's own Liberator, **Daniel O'Connell**. Receiving for their efforts little food or pay – the *raison d'être* of mercenaries – they were eventually shipped home by Bolivar who declared himself 'pleased to be rid of these vile mercenaries who would do no killing until they had been paid for it'.

## MHAOIL, GRÁINNE (1530– c. 1603)

'Grace of the cropped hair'. Also known as Granuaile or Grace O'Malley. Gráinne Mhaoil was a west of Ireland Queen of the Seas and pirate who was based on Clare Island (6.25 square miles) in Clew Bay, Co. Mayo. She is thought to have been only 15 when she married her first husband, Donal O'Flaherty. When summoned to the court of Elizabeth I in 1593, Grace displayed her mastery of the waters by sailing right around the southern coasts of Ireland and England and up the Thames into London. On other occasions she is said to have sailed as far as the Mediterranean.

Another Irish pirate queen, Anne Bonney, was commemorated on a stamp issued in Grenada in 1970.

## MIDNIGHT COURT, THE

*Cúirt an Mheán Oiche,* or 'The Midnight Court', was written in 1780 and published in 1800. A bawdy satire on Irish sexual life, it runs to almost 1200 lines. The author, Brian Merriman (1740–1805), was a schoolmaster and farmer who was born in Ennistymon, Co. Clare, the town with a waterfall just off its main street.

## MILKY WAY

The spiral structure of the Milky Way galaxy at one time could be seen only from Birr, Co. Offaly. It was here from 1850 to 1890 that astronomers came to view the heavens through the Great Telescope in the observatory of Birr Castle, the only telescope strong enough to provide the view at the time. William Parsons (1800–67), the third Earl of Rosse, had constructed the telescope and with it he made observations of distant nebulae, or star clusters.

## MOLE

William III (1650–1702), otherwise known as William of Orange, who defeated the army of King James at the Battle of the Boyne in 1690, died in 1702 when his horse stumbled in a mole hole.

## MOORE, GEORGE AUGUSTUS (1852–1933)
Co. Mayo-born novelist whom Henry 'Chips' Channon described as 'that old pink, petulant walrus', and of whom Oscar Wilde said: 'He leads his readers to the latrine and locks them in.'

## MOORE, THOMAS (1779–1852)
Dublin-born composer and poet. After the publication of the now famous *Irish Melodies* Moore became a very wealthy man. However, his hugely popular poem, *Lalla Rookh*, for which he enjoyed celebrity status and considerable financial return, is almost completely forgotten today.

(See **Pistols, Duelling**)

## MORRISON VISA
Entry permit to the United States granted by lottery.

## MOSCOW
A now vanished village in south Laois/north Kilkenny, one of a number of such settlements established by miners during the early part of the century. Such settlements were known as 'Little Moscows' because they were hotbeds of socialism.

One Irish socialist who did much to forge links between Moscow (Russia) and Ireland was Nixie Boran from Castlecomer, Co. Kilkenny. Despite the notoriety, denouncements from the pulpit and strict border security, he managed to visit Russia for the Red International of Labour Unions in August 1930 and bring home first-hand knowledge of workers' organizations.

Moscow is also the name of one of the bedrooms in Mount Stewart House in Newtownards, Co. Down. The others are named after St Petersburg, Rome and Madrid.

George Count de Browne (1698–1772) was a Limerick man, who became a mercenary and eventually a general in the Russian army, commanding some 30,000 men.

## MOTORCAR

Despite the fact that John Rowan (1787–1858) invented a steam-driven vehicle which was later claimed as a motorcar, Dr John F. Colohan in 1896 drove Ireland's first vehicle we would recognize as a motorcar and not a steam-car, a 1/2 H.P. Benz C.

The first 'automobile' accident seems to have been the death of Lady Bangor, through a fall from a steam-car made by Charles Parsons (1854–1931), using tools from his father's workshop. Parsons also invented the auxetophone, a device which amplified the sound of stringed instruments.

And, also in a musical vein, Richard Pockrich or Puckeridge (1690–1759), from Monaghan, invented, among other things, a system of filling glasses with liquid so that they produced musical notes, as well as a new form of dulcimer, and Charles Cligget (1740–95), from Waterford, invented a two-headed guitar with 18 strings. But none of these was as enduring as the motorcar.

## MOUNTJOY

A Dublin prison.

Also the name of the ship which broke the blockading boom to lift the siege of Derry on 18 July 1689 (old calendar), after 238 days.

(See **Aircraft**)

## MOUSE

St Canice of Kilkenny banished rats and mice in much the same fashion as St Patrick banished snakes, but with less success. St Kevin, however, had a mouse who was a close friend.

(See **Shirty**; **Whooping Cough**)

## MULLINGAR

This midland town was the location of the first ever Fleadh Cheoil or Irish music festival in the late 1960s.

General R.E.H. Dyer, the officer responsible for the massacre at Amritsar, India in 1919, though born in the Punjab, was educated at Mullingar's Middleton College.

(See **Reincarnation**; **Amputation**)

## MUMPS

A cure for the mumps is to take a child afflicted with them to a pigsty and rub him up and down against the back of a pig in the hope that the mumps will pass to the animal.

## MÜNCHAUSEN, BARON

Traveller and liar, hero of the fantastic novel *The Travels and Adventures of Baron Münchausen* (1785), Münchausen was the creation of Rudolf Ehrich Raspe (1737–94) who died and is buried in Killarney, Co. Kerry.

## MURDER

According to Sir Walter Scott in 1825, the Irish 'are terribly excitable to be sure and will murder you on slight suspicion, and find out next day that it was all a mistake, and that it was not yourself they meant to kill, at all at all.'

One famous murder case in recent Irish history concerned a dismembered body which had been boiled and hidden about the flat of Shan Mohangi, a young Indian from South Africa living in Dublin. In 1963 Mohangi was found guilty of murder and was sent to prison. Ten years later he was released and returned to Natal, where he became an elected public representative.

(See **GUBU**; **Wallets**; **Frankenstein**; **Pigs**)

**NAVAN**
Backwards town in Co. Meath.

**NELSON, HORATIO VISCOUNT (1758–1805)**
5 foot 2 inches of British sailor, Nelson first lost an eye and then most of his right arm in battle in the space of four years. His likeness by Thomas Kirk atop a column in Dublin's O'Connell Street, 168 steps up, was inaugurated in 1808, even before Nelson's Column in London. It was destroyed by the IRA with a bomb on 8 March 1966. A clock nearby in O'Connell Street was stopped by the blast – 1.32 am – though there was little damage to surrounding buildings. The subsequent clean-up and removal of the 'stump' did, however, cause considerable damage.

Kirk was also the sculptor responsible for the famous Metal Man in Tramore, Co. Waterford, and the figures of Mercury, Fidelity and Hibernia on the façade of Dublin's **GPO**.

**NESSIE**
The fabled monster of Scotland's Loch Ness. **St Columba** came across him/her/it in AD 565 when he/she/it was about to dine on an unfortunate swimmer. Columba dismissed the beast, which he called

Niseag, with the words: 'Go thou no further nor touch the man. Go back at once.' And Nessie obeyed.

## NEWGRANGE
Passage grave and solar calendar situated on the banks of the Boyne in Co. Meath, and dating from about 3000 BC. Newgrange, which is approximately 40 feet high and nearly 300 feet in diameter, with a 62 foot passageway, is considered by many to be one of the oldest extant 'rooms' in the world, predating the pyramids of Egypt by at least 500 years.

## NEWT
*Triturus vulgaris*. The newt is the only reptile indigenous to Ireland, all others having been driven out by a combination of **St Patrick** and the various ice ages.

## NEWTOWNMOUNTKENNEDY
Believed by many to be the longest place name in Ireland, except by those who have heard of Muickeenachidirdhashaile ('soft place between two seas') in Co. Galway, or Castletownconyersmaceniery in Co. Limerick.

## NO
An English word for which there is no direct Irish equivalent. This is due to the fact that, in Irish, a negative can only be given by the negative form of the verb. This explains what, for the visitor, appears an annoying and peculiarly Irish habit, that of returning a roundabout answer to a simple question. E.g. 'Was that you I saw yesterday on the way to work with a shovel over your shoulder and a cigarette in your mouth?' Answer: 'It was not me you saw yesterday on the way to work with a shovel over my shoulder and a cigarette in my mouth.'

(See **Yes**)

## NOAH

The famous Annals of the Four Masters, which were compiled in AD 1616 in an abbey near Bundoran, Co. Donegal, recount the history of Ireland from 2958 BC. The first entry tells of the visit of Cesara, a grand-daughter of Noah, 40 years before the Great Flood.

In the Middle Ages it was 17 March that was traditionally regarded as the day when Noah, his family and the animals entered the ark.

St Patrick's Day, 1904, saw a solar eclipse.

## NOBEL PRIZE

Three Dubliners have received the Nobel Prize for Literature: **W.B. Yeats** in 1923, **George Bernard Shaw** in 1925 and **Samuel Beckett** in 1969. The Nobel Peace Prize was twice awarded to Irish citizens, to Sean MacBride in 1974 and to Mairead Corrigan and Betty Williams jointly in 1976. The Nobel Prize for Physics was awarded to Ernest Walton in 1951.

Though he never won the Nobel Prize for Literature, the poet **Patrick Kavanagh** was born on the 71st anniversary of Alfred Nobel's birthday.

## NOISE

Apart from physical differences between the Irish and their near neighbours, the Frenchman Paschal Grousset, writing as Philippe Dacyl in his 1888 book, *Ireland's Disease* (London), identified the following: 'Still more different from the English is the inner man; naturally mirthful and expansive, witty, careless, even giddy, quarrelsome from mere love of noise, prompt to enthusiasm or despondency...'. He also went on to even more elaborate claims: 'He is the Frenchman of the West, as the Pole or Japanese are Frenchmen of the East.'

## NOSES

(See **Vikings**)

## NUCLEAR REACTION

The first nuclear reaction brought about through artifically accelerated particles, and without the aid of any form of natural radioactivity, was conducted by Dungarvan-born physicist Ernest Walton (b. 1903) with Sir John Douglas Cockfort, earning them the Nobel Prize for Physics in 1951.

## NUDITY

Founded in Dublin on 1 May 1843 by Joshua Jacob (1805–77), the White Quakers was a sect dedicated to conformity and simplicity. One of its first rules was that members must wear only undyed garments, because flashy colours and individual dressing were disapproved of. Under Jacob's guidance, this primary rule became an obsession and, following the example of Solomon Eccles, who in London had destroyed his musical instruments and run through the streets naked, bemoaning the fate of the city, the White Quakers organized a nude procession through the streets of Dublin, during which members destroyed anything ornamental or pleasure-seeking they came across en route. It was some time after this episode that Joshua began to have the increasingly bizarre visions for which he is justifiably famous. One involved a wild elephant which he had to attempt to restrain with boat ropes on the quays of his native Clonmel, Co. Tipperary. Jacob converted to Catholicism after the death of his wife, Abigail.

The only official nudist bathing place in Ireland is the Forty Foot at Sandycove, Co. Dublin. It is visible from the Martello Tower, where Joyce set the opening scene of *Ulysses*.

## O'BRIEN, FLANN (1911–66)

Real name Brian O'Nolan. Aka Myles na gCopaleen. Aka George Knowall. Born in Tyrone, the third eldest of twelve children, O'Brien worked in Dublin as a civil servant while writing the comic masterpieces *At Swim-Two-Birds* (1939), *The Hard Life* (1961), *The Dalkey Archive* (1964) and *The Third Policeman* which was written in 1940 but not published until 1967. His only novel in Irish was *An Béal Bocht* (1941), translated as *The Poor Mouth*. He also wrote a number of second-rate detective novels as well as contributing a column, 'An Cruiskeen Lawn', to the *Irish Times*. Arguably Ireland's premier humorist, he died, fittingly, on April Fool's Day, 1966.

## O'CASEY, SEAN (1880–1964)

Real name John Casey. Playwright of such classics as *The Shadow of a Gunman* (1923), *Juno and the Paycock* (1924) and *The Plough and the Stars* (1926), all of which have in recent years been prescribed texts for secondary school examinations. O'Casey left school at the age of nine.

(See **Hair**; **Eyes**)

## O'CONNELL, DANIEL (1775–1847)

'The Liberator'. Irish-speaker who advocated the use of the English language in the interest of progress and out of loyalty to the crown. Born in Carhen, Co. Kerry, he was described in a contemporary edition of *The Times* of London as: 'Scum condensed of Irish bog/Ruffian, coward, demagogue,/Boundless liar, base detractor,/Nurse of murderers, treason's factor.'

O'Connell's grandfather, Domhnaill Mor O'Connaill, was the father of Eibhlin Dhubh Ni Chonaill (1748–1800), author of the famous *Caoineadh Airt Ui Laoghaire* or 'The Lament for Art O'Leary'. She was one of a family of 22.

(See **Stonehenge**)

## O'CONNELL STREET, DUBLIN

Dublin's main thoroughfare was once called Sackville Street. At the end of it is the O'Connell monument, unveiled on 15 August 1882. The Frenchman Paschal Grousset, in his book *Ireland's Disease* (London, 1888), had this to say about the centre of the city: 'What gives the principal streets of Dublin their peculiar character is the perpetual presence at every hour of the day of long rows of loiterers... As in Naples they stop there by hundreds; some in a sitting position or stretched at full length on the bare stone, others standing with their backs to the wall, all staring vaguely in front of them, doing nothing, hardly saying more... absorbed in the dull voluptuousness of inaction... [Their] normal function is to be idle, to hem as a human fringe the public monuments.'

## O'DONNELL, DANIEL (b. 1961)

Donegal-born Country and Irish star who is the victim of many unfair jokes and much character assassination. Such as: 'Did you hear about the fellow who went into the Virgin Megastore in Dublin and bought a packet of condoms? He was too embarrassed to ask for a Daniel O'Donnell record.'

Whatever about condoms, O'Donnell has sold almost a million records to date.

Donegal means 'Fortress of the Foreigners'.

## OGHAM

Ancient Irish alphabet (4th to 7th century) consisting of 20 characters, often found on Ogham Stones which are thought to have stood as memorials to those named thereon.

The patriot **Robert Emmet** could repeat the standard English alphabet backwards without pausing.

The familiar two-colour lined school copybook in which Irish children perfected their letters was designed by Vere Foster (1819–1900).

## O'HIGGINS, BERNARDO (1778–1842)

Irish founder of the Chilean navy and father of Chilean independence, O'Higgins was also the President of Chile from 1818 to 1823. He was born of a Chilean mother and an Irish father who came from Co. Meath, and who at one stage had himself been Viceroy of Peru. It is his famous son, however, that O'Higgins Province in Chile is named for.

## OLDEST

The oldest Irish person whose dates can be certified was Katherine Plunkett. She was born on 22 November 1820 and died on 14 October 1932, aged 111 years, 326 days. If she had lived until the age of 143, she would have seen **John F. Kennedy** assassinated on her birthday.

St Kevin, if the records can be believed, died at the age of 120 in AD 618.

## OLYMPICS

Ronnie Delany was the first ever Olympic gold medal winner for Ireland, in the 1500 metres at the

Melbourne Games in 1956. Incredibly, before this, eighteen people who had been born in Ireland but were competing for other countries, had collected the gold. In fact, in the hammer throw alone, seven of the first eight gold medals won after its introduction in 1900 went to athletes born in Ireland.

The euphoria experienced by Delany's win for his own country seems to have been felt as far away as North Korea where a postage stamp of his historic feat (no pun intended) was issued. However, in their excitement, they managed to misspell his name. The Dominican Republic, later, got it right.

## ORANGE ORDER
A Protestant political body, its precursor was the Peep O'Day Boys which was formed in the 1780s and whose members were so called because they favoured early morning for their sectarian activities.

## Ó RATHAILLE, AODHAGÁN (1670–1726)
Bard. Little is known of the Kerry-born poet's life except that he lived and died in poverty and left a number of the finest vision poems, or *aislingí*, in the language.

## OSCAR
Academy Award of the American motion picture industry. The famous statuette was designed in 1927 by Dublin-born art director Cedric Gibbons, who himself won twelve of the things in a period of 27 years. As to the name, the story goes that a secretary thought Gibbons's design for the statuette looked like her Uncle Oscar, and the name stuck.

(See **Shaw, George Bernard**)

## PADDY

An Irish first name for males.

An Irish whiskey.

Also a derogatory name for any Irishman, believed to have been first used on the stage by Richard Head in *Hic et Ubique or The Humours of Dublin* (1663).

The last words of British building tycoon, Sir Arthur MacAlpine (MacAlpine's Fusiliers) were purported to be: 'Keep Paddy behind the big [cement] mixer.'

## PAISLEY, REV. IAN (b. 1926)

Ulster Presbyterian churchman and MP who remarked in 1974 on the then Pope, 'We do not accept the word of the slanderous bachelor who lives on the banks of the Tiber.'

## PALE, THE

An area around Dublin, stretching as far north as Dundalk, beyond which the decrees of Parliament had little effect. The phrase 'beyond the Pale' has come to mean barbarous and ungovernable.

### PARNELL, CHARLES STEWART (1846–91)

Wicklow-born reformer and democrat, and founder with Michael Davitt of the Land League, who was cited for adultery in 1890, causing him to lose the leadership of his Home Rule party. A year later he was dead.

(See **Love**; **Gold**; **Typhoid**)

### PATRICK, SAINT (c. 415–492)

Patron saint of Ireland and of French fishermen. Actually Patrick was a Roman Briton, probably born near the River Severn or on the island of Anglesey. He has gone down in history as the evangelizer of the Irish who is said to have come to Ireland as a slave in AD 432, escaping and returning again to drive out snakes, lecture on the shamrock and climb a variety of mountains. Patrick's feast day, 17 March, is celebrated by parades the world over, though Newfoundland is the only other place outside of Ireland where the day is celebrated as an official holiday.

Another Patrick who spent time in the northern county of Down – in fact he was born there before moving to England – was Patrick Brontë, the father of the famous novelist sisters, Emily ('a little bit of a creature without a pennyworth of good looks' – William Makepeace Thackeray), Charlotte ('a coarse, brilliant, selfish waif' – Angus Easson) and Anne ('a sort of literary Cinderella' – George Moore). Patrick Brontë was so called because he was born on the saint's feast day in 1777.

(See **Playboy**; **Noah**)

### PEARSE, PATRICK (1879–1916)

Poet and republican who was born in Dublin the year the Virgin Mary is reported to have appeared at Knock, and who lived for a time in a cottage in Rosmuck, Connemara. Pearse was among those executed on 3 May for his part in the 1916 Easter Rising.

He had said, jokingly, in the spring of that year: 'If we do nothing else we shall rid Ireland of three bad poets.' He was referring to Thomas McDonagh (1878–1916), Joseph Mary Plunkett (1887–1916) and himself.

### PEEL, SIR ROBERT (1788-1850)
Chief Secretary for Ireland from 1812 to 1818. Nicknamed Orange Peel for his anti-Catholic proclivities, Peel established the Queen's Colleges for non-sectarian higher education and continually offered criticisms of the Whigs's Irish policies. In 1814 he established the Royal Irish Constabulary, the world's first organized police force, hence the word 'peeler'.

### PENAL LAWS
A system of laws introduced in 1695 to ensure against Catholic resurgence.

(See **Wheels**)

### PETER PAN
Herbert Brenon, the film director who made *Peter Pan* and *Beau Geste*, was born in Dun Laoghaire in 1880.

The stage version of *Peter Pan* premiered in London on 27 December 1904, the same day the Abbey Theatre opened in Dublin for the first time.

(See **Acting**)

### PHOENIX PARK
At some 1760 acres, the Phoenix Park is the largest enclosed park in the world. Established by the Duke of Ormond about 1662, it has been a public park since 1745 and is the pride of Dubliners. The central thoroughfare is illuminated by gas lamps, hand-and-taper lit at night. The park is also home of Aras an

Uachtarain, a private house built in 1751 which became the Presidential Palace when **Douglas Hyde** moved there in 1938. The park also houses the Zoological Gardens (1831), the American Ambassador's residence and St Mary's Hospital, and was the site of the largest of Pope John Paul II's masses during his 1979 visit to Ireland.

(See **GUBU**)

## PHOTOGRAPHS
The celebrated photographs of the American Civil War of 1861, in which thousands of Irish fought and died on both sides, were taken by Mathew Brady whose parents came from Cork.

(See **Kavanagh, Patrick**)

## PIANOS
Cases marked 'piano' in the Dublin docks area at the end of the 18th century were to be avoided. A Scots naval surgeon called William Rae used them to smuggle cadavers across the water.

## PIGS
In his novel, *An Béal Bocht* or *The Poor Mouth*, **Flann O'Brien** hilariously describes a hard time with an over-fed pig stuck in a house, but it was Princess Margaret who said to Irish Mayor Jane Byrne at a dinner in Chicago in October 1979, after the murder by the IRA of Lord Mountbatten: 'The Irish, they're pigs.' And then, realizing her blunder, she spluttered: 'Oh, oh! You're Irish!'

In 1988 there were 960,200 pigs in Ireland. Which seems like a lot, especially when one considers that the father of the famous bushranger and outlaw, Ned Kelly, was deported to Australia for stealing just two.

(See **Communism**; **Mumps**)

## PINEAPPLES

'Pineapple rock, lemon platt, butter scotch. A sugar-stick girl shovelling scoopfuls of creams for a christian brother. Some school treat. Bad for their tummies.' So begins a section of Joyce's *Ulysses*, set in Dublin in 1904. But, though the climate hardly brings pineapples to mind, the fruit had been grown there as early as the 1750s.

The grower was a professional gardener called John Phelan who cultivated pineapples in his specially constructed glasshouses in Harold's Cross. Phelan's accomplishment is all the more noteworthy when one considers that pineapples require a root soil temperature of 75°F, and it was only through a long process of applying rotting material to the soil that he managed to raise the heat sufficiently.

Someone who appreciated his efforts, if not the pineapples themselves, was one John Hall who was apprehended in the process of stealing large quantities of them and who, after serving a sentence in Newgate Gaol in Dublin, was probably transported.

The thief out of the way, Phelan was now free to work on other projects and proved himself something of a topiarist also, cutting his hedges into the forms of birds and animals.

## PISTOLS, DUELLING

In 18th-century Irish taverns it was the custom to keep duelling pistols behind the bar for the convenience of those customers who wanted to settle their arguments on the spot. The patriot **Henry Grattan**, for instance, shot and wounded one Isaac Corry in a duel on 15 January 1800.

Duelling with swords was also very popular but, according to an account from dismissed judge and historian Jonah Barrington (1760–1834): 'No young fellow could finish his education till he had exchanged shots with some of his acquaintances.'

At length the practice of duelling was somewhat tamed by the formation of fencing clubs, one of the first of which, The Knights of Tara, met in Capel Street, Dublin. However, Jonah Barrington was soon despairing over the Knights' dress sense, and described them as 'contemptible groups of smirking quadrillers with unweaponed belts, stuffed breasts, and strangled loins! – a set of squeaking dandies, whose sex may be readily mistaken, or, I should say, is of no consequence'.

The oldest drinking house in Ireland is the Brazen Head in Dublin, dating back as far as the 12th century and possibly earlier. The present building, however, was established only in 1668, though this still makes it Dublin's oldest inn. However, though no pistols survive for the pleasure of arguing customers, the Brazen Head was once a popular meeting spot for potential insurgents and rebels. It is said that in one year alone more than 15 conspiring United Irishmen were arrested there.

The poet Thomas Moore was once prevented from proceeding with a duel against a reviewer who criticized his *Epistles, Odes and Other Poems*. Luckily for someone, it was found that only one of the pistols was loaded and the duel was called off.

## PLANTATION

The systematic replacement of natives by foreigners first introduced in Laois and Offaly in 1556 and then in Ulster in the early years of the 17th century. Though plantation was, in the main, the removal of native Catholics and the substitution of Protestant settlers, it was not only the Catholics who suffered. 'When the government took steps against Ulster Presbyterian ministers, their congregations would row across to worship in Scotland, returning the same evening' – *Modern Ireland 1600–1972*, R.F. Foster.

## PLAYBOY

Apart from *Playboy* and *Penthouse*, many books and periodicals available in the UK have been banned in Ireland. Among the books banned during the 1970s for periods of 12 years were: Gore Vidal's *The City and the Pillar*, Luke Rhinehart's *The Dice Man*, Mickey Spillane's *The Erection Set*, Erica Jong's *Fear of Flying*, Jean Genet's *Funeral Rites*, Charles Bukowski's *Notes of a Dirty Old Man* and William Burroughs's *The Naked Lunch*. Any good bookshop should now have them.

Also banned, however, were such titles as *Adam and Evil*, *All the Broads I Want*, *Animal Sex Among Housewives*, *The Anthology of Spanking Literature*, and *The Oral Game* by one Dick Mountain. These should still be pretty hard to find.

The *News of the World* newspaper was banned in Ireland until a special Irish edition was prepared in 1961 (the year **St Patrick** was adopted as the second national saint of Nigeria).

Among publications still banned are *Penthouse*, *Psychology* (!) and, fittingly, a magazine called *Suppressed*.

## PLAYBOY OF THE WESTERN WORLD, THE

The title of a play by John Millington Synge.

(See **Shift**)

## PNEUMATIC TYRE

Invented by Dubliner John Dunlop (1840–1921).

## POETS LAUREATE

There have been two Irish-born Poets Laureate of England. The first was Nahum Tate (1652–1715), who was appointed in 1692 and who is probably best remembered as the author of 'While Shepherds Watched their Flocks by Night'. Tate's father bore the given name Faithful.

The second Irish Poet Laureate was Cecil Day-Lewis (1904-72), the father of actor Daniel Day-Lewis. Both Poets Laureate were the sons of clergymen. Day-Lewis also wrote detective novels under the pseudonym Nicholas Blake.

(See **Shakespeare, William**)

## PÓG MÓ THÓIN
A popular Irish insult.

This was also the original name of the first generation London traditional/rock group The Pogues, originally led by Shane McGowan who was later relieved of his duties to be replaced by ex-Clash frontman, Joe Strummer. *Póg mó thóin* means 'kiss my arse'.

## POITÍN/POTEEN
Popular, illegal and certainly, in large quantities, deadly spirit made from a variety of plants including the potato.

A bottle with two necks is called a Wolfe's Bottle after its inventor Peter Wolfe (c. 1727–1803) who came from Limerick, but it is used in science laboratories and is not generally associated with *poitín*.

## POLES
Co. Kildare man Sir Ernest Shackleton (1874–1922) came to within 97 miles of the South Pole in 1907, and while there edited the first periodical produced in the Antarctic, the *South Polar Times*. But it was Wexford-born explorer Robert John le Mesurier M'Clure (1807–73) who was among the party that discovered the North-West Passage at the other frozen end of the globe in 1848.

The Kelvin Scale for measuring temperature was devised by William Thompson Kelvin (1824–1907) who was born in Belfast. He was also the man who discovered the celebrated Second Law of Thermodynamics.

(See **Noise**)

## POPES

St Killian, said to have been the only Irishman ever offered the Papacy, refused. However, popes from various countries have been intimately involved in the history of Ireland.

Adrian IV, for instance, whose real name was Nicholas Brakespear, and who was the only ever English pope (1154–9), felt inclined to grant the 'hereditary possession of Ireland' to Henry II of England, in 1155 in a papal privilege known as the *Laudabiliter*, arguably beginning the political troubles that continue to this day. (Incidentally, Pope Adrian VI – no relation – choked to death on a fly in his drinking water.)

A pope who gave something to Ireland, rather than giving Ireland to someone, was Paschal II who, in 1110, gave what was believed to be a splinter of the True Cross on which Christ had been crucified to the King of Munster. The splinter ended up in Thurles where it can be seen to this day in Holy Cross Abbey, which was founded in 1180.

(See **John Paul II, Pope**)

## PORTER

Doorman – black with white head.

## PORTLAOISE

Home of Ireland's main maximum security political prison. *The Rough Guide to Ireland*, 1990, says: 'The main road by-passes it entirely, and unless you arrive by train and can't avoid it, you're probably well advised to do the same.'

(See **Submarines**; **Eyes**)

## POTATO

According to Augustus Hare in his 1827 *Guesses at Truth*, 'Every Irishman... has a potato in his head.'

A plant of the genus *Solanum*, or nightshade family, the potato was introduced to Ireland by Sir Walter Raleigh in the 16th century. It came from Peru where its poisonous properties (when underripe) are known to have caused widespread epidemics of solanine poisoning. In fact, the potato was first offered as a foodstuff to the Spanish invaders of South America in the hope that it would poison them and so put an abrupt end to their plans for conquest.

In Ireland the potato soon became the staple diet, though originally it was eaten only until 17 March (St Patrick's Day). Its failure due to a blight was the cause of the Great Famine of the late 1840s in which the population of Ireland was virtually halved.

In **Shakespeare**'s *The Merry Wives of Windsor* (Act V, Scene 5) Falstaff says 'Let the sky rain potatoes', even though potatoes had not yet been introduced to these islands at the time the play was set.

(See **Famine**; **Poitín**)

## PREGNANCY

While he was alive, Cork-born James Miranda Barry (b. 1799) attracted much attention and gossip due to his close friendships with other men. His relationship with Lord Somerset drew no small amount of speculation as to the activities of this surgeon of the British Navy and one-time medical officer to Napoleon. However, it was only when Barry died, after a career which saw him promoted to Surgeon General – having served in Jamaica, Malta and St Helena – that it was discovered he was a she. This at least went some way to explaining the fact that Barry had some time earlier given birth.

## PRETENDER

Having been crowned King of England in May 1487 at Christ Church, Dublin, taking the name Edward VI, the Pretender Lambert Simnel, two weeks later, organized the first Irish invasion of England. His troops landed on the Lancashire coast and were met by the armies of Henry II at Stoke where 4000 fell before Simnel was taken captive. According to some sources Lambert spent the remainder of his life as a kitchen-hand in the royal scullery.

## PRIEST

A reverend of the Catholic Church.

Priests, especially with the introduction of the Penal Laws in 1695, had a hard time of it. Often, to avoid persecution, they were forced to celebrate mass in forests at remote mass rocks.

When the writer Liam O'Flaherty (1897–1984) discovered he no longer had a calling for the priesthood, he left university and joined the British Army.

Oliver Cromwell used Inishbofin off the west coast as a place to keep troublesome priests. Inishbofin means 'Island of the White Cow'.

(See **Stonehenge**; **Wheels**)

## PRIME MINISTERS

There have been many Irish-born Prime Ministers of foreign countries.

Arthur Wellesley, better known as the **Duke of Wellington**, is the only Irish-born Prime Minister of Britain to date, having served from 1828 to 1830.

William Ferguson Massey, who came from Derry, went on to become Prime Minister of New Zealand, 1912–25.

John Ballance from Antrim also held the position, 1891–3.

British Prime Ministers live at 10 Downing Street (named after 17th-century Dublin-born politician, Sir

Charles Downing), so it was here that incensed Boyle, Co. Roscommon woman Margaret Cousins (1878–1954) came to throw stones to vent her anger at sexual inequality, earning her a six-month sentence in prison. Cousins afterwards, in 1915, went to India where she worked for women's rights and became the first woman magistrate in that country, though she never achieved the rank of Prime Minister.

## PROLIFIC
Katherine Tynan Hinkson (1861–1931), the Dublin-born writer who died in 1931, wrote 18 collections of poetry and 12 of short stories, as well as volumes of criticism, assorted essays and memoirs.

Oh – and 105 novels as well.

## PROSPEROUS
Robert Brooke who founded the Co. Kildare town of Prosperous died in utter poverty.

Richard Brinsley Sheridan (1751–1816) also died in poverty. 40 years earlier, in 1776, the playwright and politician, who had a habit of working through the night, surrounded by candles and eating toasted muffins, had been able to buy half of Drury Lane Theatre for the then enormous sum of £35,000.

## PTOLEMY
A Greek astronomer and geographer who worked in Alexandria in the 2nd century BC, Ptolemy rated Ireland (Hibernia) as the fourth largest island in the known world.

Even while it was still almost unknown in Imperial Rome, Greek was widely spoken by Irish clerics.

## PURCELL, NOEL (1900–85)
Fondly remembered as Ireland's Father Christmas. Actor, singer and raconteur Noel Purcell, himself born two days before Christmas, made his stage debut as

the back end of a donkey, progressing to many famous films, including *Mutiny on the Bounty* with Marlon Brando, as well as countless comedies and biblical epics.

The last survivor of the real mutiny on the *Bounty*, which took place in 1789, was John Adams who came from Derry.

## PURSER, SARAH (1848–1943)

Sarah Purser is well-known for her portraits of Eva Gore-Booth and **Countess Markievicz**. A stong-willed woman, she was almost 90 years of age when she persuaded **Oliver St John Gogarty** to fly her in his plane over Mespil House in Dublin so that she might inspect the roof.

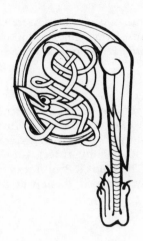

There is no Q in the Irish alphabet.

## QUARE FELLOW, THE
(See **Behan, Brendan**)

## QUARE WAN
Dublin expression for a peculiar female, often elderly.
Also an affectionate term for a girlfriend or wife.

## QUARK
Smallest elementary particle of the new theoretical
science of matter, the quark is named after a line in
Joyce's *Finnegan's Wake*: 'Three quarks for Muster
Mark!'

## QUEENSBERRY, MARQUESS OF
(See **Wilde, Oscar**)

## QUIET MAN, THE
A film by John Ford shot in Cong, Co. Mayo, and starring John Wayne and Maureen O'Hara.

'The quiet Irishman is about as harmless as a powder magazine built over a match factory' – James Dunne, *The Penguin Dictionary of Modern Quotations*, 1971.

## QUINN, BOB
Writer and film-maker whose book and television series *Atlantean* examines ancient links between Africa and Ireland through its investigations of music, language and social convention, and whose film *Budawanny* (lit. 'The Monk's Penis') was recently reissued in a slightly changed version as *The Bishop's Story*.

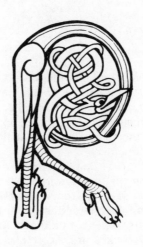

## RAJAH FROM TIPPERARY
Known as the 'Rajah from Tipperary', George Thomas (1756–1802) was born in Roscrea, Co. Tipperary, and received his nickname for his adventures in India where, in 1797, he managed to seize power and become the effective ruler of an area which had revenues in excess of £200,000.

## RARE AUL' TIMES
Mythical past in which the grass was green and pigs could fly.

When grass is not green but bleached and dried by the sun it is called hay. The wrestler Giant Haystacks, whose real name is Luke McMasters, was born in 1947, and it was on his tenth birthday that the rare aul' times could be said to have come to an end. For it was on 10 October 1957 that there was a major leak of radioactive material at the **Windscale** nuclear power plant in Cumbria, England.

When pigs are not flying, or contaminated from nearby radioactive leaks, their blood may be extracted and mixed with cream and salt to form the traditional black pudding of Cork, known as *drisheen*.

## RATS

There are no rats on Tory Island off the coast of Donegal, despite regular traffic with the mainland and all too frequent maritime accidents in the region. According to tradition, St Columcille banished all the rats in the 6th century, and there supposedly remains something in the soil of Tory that makes it impossible for rats to return.

It is said that an Englishman who once tested the notion by importing rodents from the mainland found that no sooner had his rodent friends alighted than they upped and died. Giraldus Cambrensis, writing in the 12th century, cites an unknown quality of the soil as the reason snakes and other poisonous creatures cannot live in Ireland.

Other methods for getting rid of rats are to send them a letter or to place a razor blade in an open space and begin to read aloud from the Bible. On hearing this the rats will queue up to slit their own throats.

Tory is said to have been the residence of Balor of the Evil Eye, the Celtic god of darkness.

## REAGAN, RONALD (b. 1911)

American actor and 40th President of the USA whom Gore Vidal described as 'a triumph of the embalmer's art'. In June 1984 Reagan visited his ancestral home at Ballyporeen, Co. Tipperary, from which his great-grandfather, Michael Reagan, had emigrated in 1858.

## RECTOR

Ireland's first woman rector in charge of her own parish is Rev. Kathleen Young, ordained in Belfast in June 1990 and given her appointment in October 1992.

## REINCARNATION

The only known trial of a dog which almost resulted in its hanging took place on 8 May 1860 in Mullingar. The dog, who was called Gusty, was owned by the eccentric Adolphus Cooke who suspected that Gusty and other animals around his property were, in fact, reincarnations of his father and other ancestors. The dog, having taking to wandering from the estate, much to Cooke's annoyance, was advised of the punishment that would befall him if he repeated his crime, upon which advice he duly disappeared in search of amusement. Incensed, Cooke dispatched his men to arrest the errant mutt, but one of them convinced his master that the dog had spoken to him, and Cooke, delighted finally to have independent confirmation of his reincarnation theory, ordered that the dog's life be spared.

Cooke's problems, however, were not over. Suspecting that he himself might one day return as a fox, he ordered that special trenches be dug about the estate so that in future all foxes could hide from hunters. And in a further consideration of the implications and travails of reincarnation, he had built an enormous vault in which he might be buried and in which were arranged a chair, table, quills and paper in case he should immediately want to write of his experiences after his revival. It did not seem to bother Cooke that a fox might experience considerable difficulty in trying to manipulate writing instruments. However, he was to change his mind about the venture and, in the event, the vault was never used.

After Cooke's death in 1876, his will was contested on the grounds that he had all along been insane but, suspecting trickery, in an historic ruling the judge declared 'If a man believes he will turn into a successful screech-owl after his death, that is no proof that he is incapable.' The case was dismissed.

## RELATIVITY

The Irish physicist George Francis Fitzgerald (1851–1901) did pioneering work to show that no object can move faster than the speed of light, work on which Albert Einstein would later draw.

## RESIGNATION

The practice of resigning when things get too hot is a common feature of present-day politics, but of course it has existed for centuries.

In Ireland, however, unlike in Britain, it is seldom linked with sexual indiscretion (although see **Casey, Bishop Eamonn**). The practice may have been instituted in AD 770 by King Niall Frassach, who, when his subjects were faced with widespread famine and pestilence, simply threw up his hands, threw in the towel and went off to become a monk on Iona.

## RESURRECTION

St Columba (AD 521–597), also known as Columcille, is said to have had the powers of resurrection. Born in Gartan, Co. Donegal, Columba, whose feast day is 9 June, founded monasteries at Derry, and at Durrow in Co. Laois, and later at Iona off the Scottish mainland.

While based on Tory Island off the coast of Donegal, Columba was visited by the holy children of the King of India who, on arrival after a long and arduous journey, simply dropped dead from exhaustion. Columba came to the rescue, immediately reviving them, but they stayed alive only long enough for him to give them his blessing before they all died again from exhaustion. After this it appears Columba gave up.

On another occasion, however, Columba is said to have refused to give up a book to the High King who was demanding it for himself, and there ensued a terrible battle near Drumcliff, Co. Sligo, in which 3000 people died, none of whom is Columba reported to have resurrected.

(See **Asgill, John**)

### RICE, EDMUND IGNATIUS (1762–1844)
Soon after his wife died, Callan, Co. Kilkenny-born Edmund Rice founded the Christian Brothers, a religious community that does not allow its members to wed.

### ROBIN HOOD
Robin Hood's friend and side-kick, Little John, was hanged in Arbour Hill in Dublin.

### ROBINSON, MARY, née Bourke (b. 1944)
Seventh President of the Republic of Ireland and the first female President in the history of the State, which means she is also the first woman Commander-in-Chief of the army. She was born Mary Bourke in Ballina, Co. Mayo, on 21 May 1944, and lived for a number of years in Dublin at 21 Westland Row, the birthplace of **Oscar Wilde**. The daughter of two doctors, at 25 she was the youngest ever Professor of Law at Trinity College Dublin. She had entered Trinity as a young Catholic with a special dispensation from the Church to study in a Protestant university.

### ROCKALL
An uninhabited rock north-west of Ireland, over which four countries claim jurisdiction. Rockall, which cannot sustain 'human habitation or economic life', being for all intents and purposes a lump of rock in the sea, should therefore be outside the UN convention relating to disputed territorial claims over islands. Nevertheless Britain, Iceland and Denmark all vie with Ireland over the title, ever since the Royal Navy visited in 1955 and announced the British claim.

   The competition rose to absurd heights in 1985,

when, to attempt to prove Britain's claim that Rockall was, after all, habitable, an ex-SAS man spent a full 40 days and nights on Her Majesty's service, cramped up in a reinforced box which had to be bolted to the rock. The dispute, however, continues.

## ROS, AMANDA MCKITTRICK (1860–1939)

Born near Ballynahinch, Co. Down, novelist Anna Margaret McKittrick seems to have been more enamoured of names than anything else. In marrying one Andy Ros, McKittrick not only gained an extra syllable on the end of her name, but she now also held the full name of the heroine of a popular novel of the time. So was born Amanda Malvina Fitzalan Anna Margaret McLelland McKitterick Ros. But her love of names did not end there. Soon she began to write her own novels, creating eponymous characters *Irene Iddesleigh,* *Helen Huddersfield* and *Delina Delaney,* the heroines of what have been called 'the worst novels ever written'. A sample from *Delina Delaney* will give a flavour: 'Have ever you visited that portion of Erin's plot that offers its sympathetic soil for the minute survey and scrutinous examination of those in political power, whose decision has wisely been the means before now of converting the stern and prejudiced, and reaching the hand of slight aid to share its strength in augmenting its agricultural richness?'

Notwithstanding, McKittrick Ros became something of a cult figure on account of her glorious (gloriously awful?) writing, and Aldous Huxley, for one, made strenuous efforts to see that her works remained in print.

## ROSES

The Rose of Tralee is the title given to a beauty queen elected from international aspirants in a yearly pageant hosted in the Co. Kerry town by broadcaster Gay Byrne.

William Pembroke Mulchinock wrote the words of the famous song.

The dramatist Richard Brinsley Sheridan, himself something of a charmer, is reputed to have propositioned a young woman with the following: 'Won't you come into the garden? I would like my roses to see you.'

## ROUND TOWERS
Giant phallic edifices used by monks for solitude, and to escape attacking Vikings. Round towers appear to be peculiar to Ireland and the western seaboard of Europe, thereby supporting the argument that Ireland may have been part of a large maritime trade and cultural exchange centuries before the Celts are supposed to have brought their influence here, coming overland across Europe. A particularly fine example of a round tower survives in Timahoe, Co. Laois. It is 96 feet high.

## RTE
Radio Telefís Éireann, the Irish national broadcasting service.

The first Irish broadcasting service was the Dublin Broadcasting Station which began on 1 January 1926. Its call sign, 2RN, was taken (phonetically) from the last words of the song 'Come Back to Erin'. The first broadcaster was **Douglas Hyde,** later to become first President of Ireland.

(See **Marconi**)

## RUSSELL, GEORGE WILLIAM (1867–1964)
Poet, painter and agrarian reformer, Russell adopted the pen name *AE* after a printer's error omitted the

last two letters of the word *AEon* at the end of a piece of his writing. Among his works is a translation of the *Bhagavadgita* in which he gets to declare: 'I am beauty itself among beautiful things.'

For a time Russell was a neighbour of W.B. Yeats's on Dublin's Merrion Square. It is said that they once passed each other on the street, one head up airily, the other head down gloomily, while on the way to visit each other.

*AE* became disillusioned with Ireland and moved to England 32 years after the beginning of this century. He died there a further 32 years later.

### SAFE CROSS CODE
System of crossing the road without being killed, popular among schoolchildren.

### SAINTS
(See **Scholars**)

### SAUSAGES
(See **Yeats, William Butler**)

### SAYERS, PÉIG (1873–1958)
Author of the classic book on endurance, *Péig*, Sayers had ten children, all of whom died or emigrated.

### SCHOLARS
(See **Saints**)

### SCHRÖDINGER, ERWIN (1887–1961)
Austrian physicist, famous for his notion of a 'wave function' to explain how the act of observation might influence reality. Schrödinger was the first professor at **de Valera**'s Institute for Advanced Studies, and

became an Irish citizen, living and working for 17 years in Dublin.

## SCOTI

An ancient name for the Irish, Scoti was later applied to those who settled in Pictland, today known as Scotland. The Scottish city of Edinburgh is named after an Irish nun, Edana, who founded a convent there in the 16th century.

## SEAN NÓS

Infinitely varying unaccompanied style of Irish singing.

## SELLAFIELD

(See **Windscale**)

## SEWERS

A journalist by the name of McGee was lucky, or unlucky, enough to be in New Newgate Gaol in July 1790 when there was a massive riot and escape. The prisoners exited through the sewers but McGee's report in the Dublin *Evening Post* preferred to use the term 'common necessary'.

Had it been written in 1790, and had the American author Henry Miller been alive at the time, down the 'common necessary' was where one was likely to find a copy of James Joyce's *Ulysses*. According to Miller, 'There are passages of *Ulysses* that can be read only in the toilet if one wants to extract the full flavour from them.'

Richard Long, an unpopular Co. Tipperary land-lord, was shot dead in 1820 while sitting on the toilet.

In the play *Face Licker Come Home* by the Galway poet Rita Ann Higgins, the female protagonist spends much of her time on the throne.

A four-year-old boy who found himself in court after spending only a short amount of time in the

same situation was Derek Skelly. The court heard
that the boy had developed a stammer after his little
finger was caught in a toilet door while attending a
Dublin Corporation Summer School. He was awarded
£4000 compensation.

## SEX PISTOLS
Punk rock band who were fronted by an Irishman,
Johnny Rotten, whose real name is John Lydon.

## SEXY
On **Eamon de Valera**'s return from a visit to France
as a young man, he summed up the feelings of many
Irish people when he said, 'All I can say is that sex in
Ireland is as yet in its infancy.'

The English poet, Donald Davie (b. 1922), might
have agreed: 'What I have always liked about the Irish
Republic is that it is, of all the societies that I know,
the least "sexy".'

## SHAKESPEARE, WILLIAM (1564–1616)
English poet and dramatist who created the first Irish
solider on stage with his portrait of Captain
MacMorris in *Henry V*, written during the Ulster rebellion.

The Irish-born Poet Laureate Nahum Tate
(1652–1715) specialized in the rewriting of classic
works of literature, including Shakespeare's.
Incredibly, it was Tate's version of *King Lear* that was
the accepted standard for almost 150 years! **George
Bernard Shaw** was also a major fan of the Bard of
Avon but, instead of rewriting the great man's work,
he had other desires: 'It would probably be a relief to
me to dig him up and throw stones at him.'

(See **Potato**; **Venom**; **Gout**)

## SHAMROCK

Ancient north African symbol. Symbol of Ireland and
Irishness. Trefoil. The shamrock was, at one stage,
eaten widely in Ireland, being first dipped in whiskey.
Banned as a trademark in Germany where it has been
copyrighted as an insignia for beef, the symbol graces
the façade of Government House on Montserrat in the
West Indies, an island with such a large population of
Irish descent it has been called the Emerald Isle of the
Caribbean. There the word 'Irish' is a not uncommon
surname. In Montreal, Canada, a city that claims an
estimated 500,000 people of Irish descent, the shamrock features as one of the four official symbols of the
city.

*The Shamrock or Hibernian Chronicle* was the first
Irish magazine. It was published on 15 December
1810 in New York City.

(See **Swastika**)

## SHAPELY

The real name of the Maze prison is Long Kesh. It was
in this notorious prison that the 1981 republican
hunger strikes took place. The layout of the camp is
in the form of the letter 'H'; hence the term 'H-Block'.
The camp might equally have been called the Zygal,
which is the word for something that is H-shaped.

Built by Charles II (who reigned from 1660–85),
the fortification called Charles Fort in Kenmare is
star-shaped.

The Irish first name Aoibheann or Eavan means
'lovely shape'.

## SHAW, GEORGE BERNARD (1856–1950)

Dublin-born playwright who left school at 15, Shaw
became music critic for *The Star* in 1888 writing
under the pseudonym *Corno di Basseto*. Though he
won and accepted the Nobel Prize for Literature in
1925, he refused an Oscar for the 1938 film version of

*My Fair Lady.* He also refused to contribute towards Wesley College during its centenary celebrations, sending a card which simply said: 'My curse on it'. He also rejected England's Order of Merit saying, 'it would be superfluous, as I have already conferred this order on myself.'

A founder member of CND, Shaw was made a Freeman of Dublin at the age of 90 and has been commemorated on a Romanian postage stamp. J.B. Priestley tells of meeting him in America at the Grand Canyon and 'finding him peevish and refusing to admire it or even look at it properly. He was jealous of it.' A stubborn and sometimes contrary man, he, for instance, refused to spell Shakespeare with the final 'e'. So, though he himself might write in *The Doctor's Dilemma*, 'I am a disciple of Bernard Shaw,' there were many others who felt as Henry Arthur James did when he said Shaw was 'a freakish homunculus germinated outside lawful procreation'.

(See **Tea**)

### SHEELA-NA-GIG
A carving in stone of a naked woman exposing her vulva, the Sheela-na-Gig, which has its roots in an earlier, pre-Christian religion, was once used, particularly over the doors of churches, to ward off evil. In later times, however, it caused considerable embarrassment to both clergy and laity and was often destroyed or removed. In some cases it is said to have been buried in the yards of the churches it once adorned. Symbolically this represented the burial of the old religion by the new.

### SHIFT
Undergarment. This was the word that ultimately led to the riot in the Abbey Theatre in 1907 during a performance of *The Playboy of the Western World* by John Millington Synge (1871–1909). The play, set in

Geesala, Co. Mayo, also caused riots in the US, and in Philadelphia, the year after Synge's death, the whole cast was arrested following a disturbance. Synge could have placed at least some of the blame at the feet of **W.B. Yeats**, because it was Yeats who had urged him to go to the west of Ireland in the first place and write about what he found there. On 12 February 1939, a reviewer in the *Observer*, obviously forgetting about the play's impact in the US, reconsidered the cause of the 1907 riot. 'Could it be,' he wondered, 'that the pure-minded men were guiltily conscious of having drunk the shifts off their women's backs, and dared not hear the word spoken for the shameful memory it raised in their heads?'

## SHINS
The shin-guard was invented by Roger Bresnihan, who was born in Tralee in 1881 and went on to become a noted US baseball player.

## SHINTO
The Derry-born scholar William George Aston (1841–1911) published a book on Japan's Shinto religion which, when translated into Japanese, became an officially approved textbook on the subject.

## SHIP
The largest ship ever built, a 312,000-ton tanker, was formally named by Mrs Mairin Lynch, the wife of the then Taoiseach, in Yokohama, Japan on 15 August 1968. The ship was called *Universe Ireland*.

## SHIRTY
Singer Luka Bloom's older brother, Christy Moore, Ireland's Woody Guthrie, is known affectionately as the 'Storm in a T-Shirt' after his unusual habit of wearing undershirts on stage.

However, the eccentric Robert Cooke, who died in 1726, only ever wore white linen shirts around his hometown of Cappoquin, Co. Waterford, though he was not a singer of any importance. His insistence on white also extended to the animals on his farm where only white horses and cattle were permitted. A white horse appeared on the cover of Christy Moore's best-selling album, *Ride On*.

Because a mouse who walks over a cow will leave the cow crippled, the farmer who sees this happen must remove his shirt and beat the cow with it nine times until the bad luck is driven away.

### SHIT, JAMES THE
Nickname earned by the Catholic King James II after the Battle of Aughrim in 1690, in which 7000 soldiers of the Franco-Irish army perished.

### SHORTHAND
The inventor of the international system of shorthand known as Gregg was John Robert Gregg from Co. Monaghan.

### SINN FÉIN
'We Ourselves'. Irish nationalist movement set up about 1905. Now the name of the political wing of the IRA whose chief of staff, Dan Hogan, was shot in 1941 by the FBI. Francis O'Neill (1849–1936), who was born in Bantry and became Chief of Police in Chicago, was also shot, at the age of 24, but survived for 43 years with the bullet still in his back. Sydney, Australia's Chief of Police in 1815 was a convict, Michael Dwyer (1771–1826), transported for his part in the 1798 Rebellion. The burning of the Eureka Hotel in New South Wales in 1854 by disgruntled miners was led by Laois-man Peter Lalor (1823–1889), and the password during the blockade was 'Vinegar Hill', the scene of the Wexford rebellion. In 1771, the year of Dwyer's birth, Benjamin Franklin visited Dublin on trade matters.

For years the offices of Sinn Féin and the Orange Order were side-by-side on Dublin's Parnell Square.

## SIX COUNTIES

Six of the nine counties that make up Ulster.

(See **Fat Dad**)

## SMOKING

All packets of Irish cigarettes carry a government health warning and there is evidence that fewer young males, whatever about females, are taking to smoking. However, in a 1699 pamphlet entitled *A Trip to Ireland*, Tom Brown tells of seeing men and women who were addicted to smoking and of an infant who took 'more delight in handling a tobacco pipe than a rattle'.

Frank O'Connor (1903–66), the short story writer, grew up in Douglas Street, Cork, 'over a small sweet-and-tobacco shop kept by a middle-aged lady called Wall'.

Not above or behind walls, but in the Ulster Causeway Safari park is where Peter the chimpanzee is to be found engaged in the peculiar habit of smoking. The chimp, who begs visitors for supplies, lights his own cigarettes much to the horror of his keepers who fear a fire in his bedding.

When Galway-born writer Padraig Ó Conaire (1882–1928) died in Richmond Hospital, Dublin, his only earthly belongings were tobacco, a pipe and an apple.

(See **Kennedy, John F**; **Xanthodont**)

## SMURFITS

Cardboard people.

## SNAKES

(See **Patrick, Saint**; **Newt**)

## SNEEM

A village in Co. Kerry. The following is a small selection of unusual Irish placenames: Kill, Golden, Moneygold (Sligo), Blueball (Offaly), Bilboa and **Moscow** (Laois), **Clones** (Monaghan), Siberia (Sligo), Trim (Meath), Stroove (Donegal), Inch and Loo Valley (Kerry), Oola (Limerick), Ballyhoo (Waterford), Shanghai and Geneva (Kilkenny), Gorey (Wexford) and Delphi (Mayo).

## SNIPER

In the South Armagh town of Cullyhanna, when nine people were shot by a sniper or snipers in one eighteen-month period to January 1994, the locals erected their own roadsign. It reads 'Sniper at Work'.

The first British soldier to be killed in the present 'troubles' was Robert Curtis of the 32nd Royal Artillery who was shot dead in Belfast by an IRA sniper on 6 February 1971. On 15 May of the same year the man believed to have fired the shot was himself shot dead in a gun battle with British troops in the city's Curtis Street.

One of the first casualities of the 1922–3 Civil War was a Free State sniper. A woman beat him over the head with a pot from her kitchen.

(See **Troubles**)

## SPIKES

Spike Island off Cork houses a prison in a former military barracks. At one time it was the main detention centre for young offenders and joy riders.

*The Spike* was the title of an Irish-made television series which ran in the late 1970s and which became famous for a schoolroom scene in which a youth urinated into a bottle.

The spike on the helmet of the Infantry of the Line was first introduced in 1878.

## SPRAT

A small herring-like fish. It was reported that a shower of sprats fell during a freak localized whirlwind on Achill Island during the 18th century. Other strange showers reported have included large numbers of berries falling in central Dublin in May 1867 and a shower of fish up to 2 inches long in Co. Clare in 1895.

Meanwhile, taking the notion of strange precipitations to the extreme, back in Achill, the *Parliamentary Gazeteer of Ireland* (1845) described the inhabitants' system of settlement, known as boleys, with the following: 'They reside principally in hamlets, each of which has been described as a congeries of hovels thrown indiscriminately together as if they fell in a shower from the sky.'

It is commonly said by someone who thinks he is being taken for a fool: 'Do you think I came down in the last shower?'

## ST STEPHEN'S GREEN

Dublin's city-centre green. Once a common beyond the city, Stephen's Green, as it is popularly known, was enclosed in 1663 and opened to the public in 1877. St Stephen, incidentally, was a common enough preacher who was chased beyond the city of Jerusalem and stoned to death.

A Dublin brothel keeper, Darkey Kelly, who was tried for murder in 1764, was publicly burned in this fashionable Dublin park. Just over a hundred years later, the last person to be publicly executed in the British Isles was Irishman Michael Barrett who had wrongly been accused of the Clerkenwell bombing of December 1867.

## STAMPS

The first Irishman on a foreign stamp was James David Bourchier from Limerick, a war correspondent who appeared on a Bulgarian issue in 1921.

Robert Ballagh (b. 1943), the Dublin-born ex-Showband performer turned artist, stage, stamp and coin designer once sold a guitar to Thin Lizzy bass player and singer **Phil Lynott**. More recently he has been responsible for the design of the new ten and five pound notes, the former of which features a portrait of James Joyce and an extract from *Ulysses*.

## STAR TREK

Cult sci-fi TV (and later feature film) series featuring Captain Kirk, Mr Spock et al. The offspring TV series, 'Star Trek – The Next Generation', suffered censorship at the hands of **RTE** in 1992 when the broadcasting organization declined to transmit an episode of the show set in the year 2221. The episode in question referred to a United Ireland that had been 'successfully liberated by Irish terrorists'.

## STATUES, MOVING

(See **Ballinspittle**)

## STERNE, LAURENCE (1713–68)

Clonmel, Co. Tipperary-born writer whose works include *Tristram Shandy* and *A Sentimental Journey*. Originally on the path to being a quiet country parson with the Church of England, Sterne was 'led astray' by a friend, John Hall-Stevenson, whose home address was Crazy Castle, a meeting place for wild young men, on the lines of Dublin's Hellfire Club which was founded in 1735. Under his influence, Sterne began to read and write in the Gothic pile's library, going on to produce the first volumes of *The Life and Opinions of Tristram Shandy, Gentleman*, to give it its full title, in 1760.

## STOKER, ABRAHAM 'BRAM' (1847–1912)

Dublin-born author of *Duties of Clerks in Petty Sessions in Ireland* and the somewhat more popular *Dracula*.

(See **Yeti**)

## STONEHENGE

The Co. Kildare town of Naas is among the places said to be the site of origin of the stones used for England's megalithic masterpiece where druids are reputed to have offered human sacrifice.

Kildare, incidentally, means Church of the Oakwood, and indicates that the now bare area was originally under trees.

Naas itself was the location of a duel fought by **Daniel O'Connell** in 1815, in which he killed a gentleman named d'Esterre.

The seminary at Maynooth in the same county, though not for druids but Catholic priests, was started with just 40 students a hundred years earlier, but by 1895 had become the largest in the world.

Though the practice of duelling was no longer considered acceptable in 1895, the theory that heretics deserved burning was, so anyone with an interest in Stonehenge would have been well advised to stay well away from what William Makepeace Thackeray called 'the miserable village of Maynooth'.

## SUBMARINES

The unarmed Cunard liner, *Lusitania*, was sunk by a German submarine off the Old Head of Kinsale, on 7 May 1915, with the loss of 1198 passengers and crew, including the art collector, Hugh Lane.

J.P. Holland, a Clareman who lived from 1841 to 1914, was responsible for many of the major developments of the submarine and is generally credited with being the father of the present-day version. As a Christian Brother, at one stage he taught in

Portlaoise, the county town of the most inland county in Ireland.

To say that *Lusitania* was sunk by a submarine is not of course precise. What it was sunk by was a torpedo. In a typical irony, the dirigible torpedo had been invented by another Irishman, Castlebar-born Louis Brennan (1852–1932).

However, by far the biggest Irish maritime disaster was the sinking by a German torpedo from UB 123 of the RMS *Leinster*, with the loss of 501 of its 771 passengers on 10 October 1918. The passengers included 492 servicemen, bringing the number of military casualities to far in excess of the number killed in the Easter Rising two years previously.

## SWASTIKA
Dublin laundry company named after an ancient oriental symbol of cyclic change and rebirth. The Swastika laundry continued to operate right through World War II.

## SWIFT, JONATHAN (1667–1745)
'I reckon no man is thoroughly miserable unless he be condemned to live in Ireland.' Born on 30 November, the day both **Patrick Kavanagh** and **Oscar Wilde** would die, Jonathan Swift became Dean of St Patrick's in Dublin in 1713. Though his most famous work is probably *Gulliver's Travels*, and it is indeed the only one for which he was ever paid (the sum of £200), he also wrote over 70 pamphlets under a variety of pen names which included Isaac Bickerstaff, Dr Andrew Tripe and A. Shoeboy.

It was Swift who suggested 'the carcass of a good fat child' for the preparation of 'four dishes of nutritious meat' while at the same time leaving in his will an endowment to build Dublin's first lunatic asylum. It is widely suspected that the Dean, who was something of a ladies' man (although he did say that women were 'a sort of species hardly a degree above a monkey'), may have died of a venereal affliction, sufferers of which are advised to turn to St Fiachra. This may be what George Orwell was referring to when he called him 'a diseased writer', or what William Makepeace Thackeray was referring to when he called Swift 'filthy in word, filthy in thought, furious, raging, obscene'. Tom Paulin, the Irish poet, also had a go at summing Swift up in 1983: 'Essentially he is an occasional poet who sings lightly about dandruff, drains, body-odour, dirty underclothes, and comic farts.' These are obviously qualities which are prized in Romania where Swift has been commemorated on a postage stamp.

## SWOPS
The Irish kings offered the High King of Ireland to Haakon IV of Norway in 1262 in return for his helping to rid the country of Normans. Haakon declined.

## TÁIN

Real name *Táin Bó Cuailgne* or *The Cattle Raid of Cooley*. An epic Irish poem about the ever-popular sport of cattle rustling. Rendered in a notable English version by Thomas Kinsella.

(See **Athlone**)

## TALBOT, MATTHEW (1856–1925)

The second eldest of twelve children, Talbot was working as a hodman on building sites in Dublin when, suddenly, at 28 years of age, he took the pledge to abstain from drink and, though almost illiterate, turned his mind to the works of St Augustine. More and more of his time began to be spent reading or praying on his knees. But the familiar sight of Talbot at prayer and devotion did not give any real indication of the extent of his asceticism. When he collapsed during a heatwave in June 1925, he was taken to Jervis Street Hospital where his spotless clothes were removed to reveal a large chain tightly wound around his body, with others tight about his arms and legs, having worn deep grooves in his flesh.

## TARA

A hill in Co. Meath which was the seat of the High Kings of Ireland until AD 1022, and on top of which was the **Lia Fáil**, or Stone of Destiny, where the kings were crowned. St Patrick lit a fire here. It was here too that **Daniel O'Connell** held a mass rally which, it is alleged, attracted a million people.

Tara was also the name of the homestead in the 1936 novel *Gone with the Wind*, featuring one Scarlett O'Hara who was modelled on Annie Fitzgerald Stephens, the daughter of a Tipperary-born plantation owner in Atlanta, Georgia.

## TAXMEN

Legend has it that it was the *Fir Bolg* ('Bag Men') who built the great fortification of Dun Aengus on Inishmore in the Aran Islands. They came to the west having fled their native Meath in an effort to avoid paying taxes to a local king. Dun Aengus, originally a circular fort, is now semi-circular, the ground beneath it having been eroded by the Atlantic, a 60-metre drop below.

## TD

Teachta Dála. Irish version of MP.

## TEA

George O'Dowd, better known as Boy George, once claimed to prefer tea to sex, which simply confirmed his Irishness in many eyes. Born in London to parents from Co. Tipperary, O'Dowd used his first name as a stage surname, while George Bernard Shaw, abhorring his, always preferred to be called Bernard.

Enamoured by tea since its arrival here in the second half of the 17th century, the Irish have taken it into their rituals in much the same way as have the Japanese. (Thomas Lipton, the tea merchant after whom Lipton's Tea is named, was born in Glasgow in

1850 to Irish parents.) Perhaps Boy George's best-loved hit song with the pop group Culture Club was 'Karma Chameleon' which is also to do with matters oriental, again of a quasi-spiritual nature, though there is no mention in the song of the fact that tea *caddies* are so called after the Malayan word for a unit of weight of just over one pound. Coincidentally, just over one pound (IRL£1) was the average price in Ireland of a single record at the time of the release of Culture Club's first hit.

Boy George was born on 14 June 1961. On 14 June 1904 Nora Barnacle stood up **James Joyce** on their first date.

## TEAGUE
A derogatory term for an Irish person, often used of Fenians or Republicans. The word *teague* or *taig* actually comes from *tadhg*, a poet or man in the street, and was once a popular given name. In Thomas O'Sheridan's play *The Brave Irishman* (1743), however, one recognizes it in its more familiar sense. Ragou, a Frenchman, is speaking to O'Blunder, the Irishman of the title. 'You be de Teague,' he says, 'de vile Irishman – de Potatoe face – Me not think it vort my while to notice you ... go to your own hottentot contre.'

(See **Bullshit**)

## TEDDY BEARS' PICNIC
Enduring popular song written by Jimmy Kennedy who was born in Omagh, Co. Tyrone, in 1903.

## TEETH
An act was passed in 1960 which legalized the addition of fluoride to public water supplies to help prevent dental decay. At the time there were approximately 600 dentists in Ireland, or one per 4800 of the population, and they must have expected business to

deteriorate. Traditionally, toothache had been relieved in Ireland by scooping clay from under an elder bush into the mouth, which may have caused some discolouring, not to mention discomfort.

(See **Xanthodont**; **Frogs**)

## TEMPERANCE

Fr Theobald Mathew (1790–1856), born in Cashel, Co. Tipperary, is commonly known as 'The Apostle of Temperance'. He preached widely against alcohol and his efforts are said to have considerably lessened the crime figures of his time. Signing his total pledge in 1838, he was heard to utter: 'Here goes in the name of the Lord.'

## TENNIS

A game with strong Irish connections. John Pius Boland, the first Irish person to win two Olympic gold medals, did so at tennis singles and doubles in Athens in 1896. The first World Ladies Tennis Championship took place at Fitzwilliam in Dublin in June 1897.

## TONE, THEOBALD WOLFE (1763–98)

Dublin-born leader of the United Irishmen whose wife, Matilda Witherington, was 15 years old when he married her in 1785. (They spent their honeymoon in Maynooth!) Tone set up the United Irishmen in 1791 and, for his revolutionary behaviour, inspired by the French Revolution, was imprisoned and sentenced to death. Refusing a soldier's death by firing squad, he decided to cut his own throat but cut his windpipe instead of his jugular ('I find I am but a bad anatomist') and waited a full eight days to die of his injuries on 19 November 1798.

**TORRENTIAL**
The Torrens River on which Adelaide, Australia, stands is named after Robert Torrens, soldier, politician and novelist, born near Derry in 1780.

**TORY**
The word for a conservative politician in the UK comes from the Irish *toiride* which means 'pursuer' and was originally applied to highwaymen and later to those who chased after royal power.

**TRACTORS**
The idea of combining tractor and plough in one unit came from Harry Ferguson (1884–1960), born in Hillsborough, Co. Down. Ferguson was also the first person in Ireland to fly in an aeroplane, on the last day of 1909. By the year of his death, there were as many as 43,700 tractors in Ireland. Today the figure is close to 84,000.

**TREASON**
Roger Casement (1864–1916), the Dublin-born republican who was in consular service in both Brazil and Africa, was executed for treason. He had been offered a speech written especially in his defence by **George Bernard Shaw** but refused. Instead he converted to Catholicism just days before the execution.

(See **Haw Haw, Lord**)

**TREATY, THE**
Signed on 6 December 1921 by a deputation led by **Michael Collins**, the Anglo-Irish Treaty returned 26 of the 32 counties to Irish government while leaving six under British control, a controversial settlement that led ultimately to the Civil War.

During the negotiation of the Treaty, another of the Irish deputation, Sir John Lavery, found himself staying in London's Cromwell Place, which cannot have left him feeling too optimistic. His wife, Lady Lavery, who was the face on the old one pound note, was not Irish at all but in fact an American woman by the name of Hazel Martyn. Sir John married her when he was 55 and she was 29, only slightly older than his own daughter.

Another important treaty, not only for the future of Ireland, but for all the world, was the Treaty of Versailles (28 June 1919). Therefore it had to be recorded. Dublin-born Sir William Orpen (1878–1931) was the offical war artist who got the job of painting the historic signing.

## TRICOLOUR
Green, white and orange flag of the Republic. The green represents patriotism and, by extension, Catholicism, while the Orange is seen to represent the Protestant point of view. The band of white was inserted, according to Thomas Francis Meagher, to signify 'a lasting truce' between the two. The truce, of course, did not last. After 1916 the tricolour became strongly associated with the Sinn Féin movement and the Cavan-Leitrim Railway even painted one of its engines green, white and orange in 1917 in a show of support.

However, it was only in 1803 that green became associated with patriotism. Before that date blue had been the preferred colour.

The Tricolour is flown once a year, on March 6, over Swiss public buildings to commemorate the Irish saint Fridolin.

## TRINITY COLLEGE
Famous landmark in the centre of Dublin. Before Trinity College existed, the site was home to the Priory of All Hallows, but this was suppressed by Henry VIII. It was not until the reign of Elizabeth I that the college was founded, in 1592. The express intention was that the college should strengthen the Reformation in

Ireland and, until June 1970, Irish Catholics who wished to attend Trinity were advised to seek the permission of their bishop.

On 31 June 1976 the astronaut Neil Armstrong was among a group of six prominent Americans conferred with honorary degrees at Trinity.

### TROUBLES
The first fatality of the so-called Troubles in Northern Ireland was a 70-year-old farmer, Francis McCluskey, who was struck in a melee between opposing factions outside the Orange Hall at Dungiven, Co. Derry, on 14 July 1969. It is believed McCluskey was an innocent bystander.

(See **Sniper**)

### TUATHA DÉ DANANN
Tribes of the goddess Dana or Danu, the Tuatha Dé Danann were a legendary race said to have invaded Ireland in 1896 BC.

### TYPHOID
**Charles Stewart Parnell**, the Home Rule reformer, once attended an all-girls' school in Somerset, but had to leave on contracting typhoid.

## U2

**Bono**, Larry, The Edge and Adam. Despite their strong Dublin affiliations, two of the band were actually born outside the country – The Edge in London, and Adam Clayton on the Isle of Wight.

## UFO

Unidentified Flying Object. The 11th-century Book of Glendalough relates the sighting of a great ship in the sky over Tailteann Fair from which a man descended to seize a spear which had been thrown at his craft. When the onlookers refused to release the spear, the man complained that he was drowning, at which moment he floated back into the sky like a body in water, reboarded his ship and departed. The story is recounted in section *viii* of the poem sequence 'Squarings' by Seamus Heaney.

## UILEANN PIPES

Traditional instrument referred to in Shakespeare's *The Merchant of Venice* as a 'woollen bagpipe'.

## UKELELE

Ukelele is the Hawaiian word for 'jumping flea'. The Irish writer **Padraic Colum** (1881–1972) may have been aware of this because in 1923 he was invited to compile a compendium of Hawaiian myths and literature.

## ULSTER

Nine-county province situated in the northern part of the island. The Red Hand of Ulster which appears on its flag is said to come from an episode where, in a race to reach Ulster first and claim it as his own, one of two competing warriors cut off his own arm and threw the bloody limb ahead of him to touch the soil first.

(See **Six Counties**)

## ULYSSES

When **James Joyce**'s *Ulysses* first began to appear in serial form and then in its eventual first volume publication in Paris by Sylvia Beach on 2 February 1922 (Joyce's birthday), it was met with outrage and denouncement. However, the subscribed edition of 1000 which Beach had organized attracted some distinguished patrons, one of whom was **Winston Churchill**. An American edition followed in 1934 but an Irish edition has yet to appear.

The greatest novel of all time? There are some who would disagree. **D.H. Lawrence**, for instance, was none too impressed with Joyce's offering. In a letter to Aldous Huxley in 1928, he said it was, 'Nothing but old fags and cabbage stumps of quotations from the Bible and the rest, stewed in the juice of deliberate, journalistic dirty-mindedness.' Virginia Woolf was at least more pithy. '*Ulysses* is the work of a queasy undergraduate, scratching his pimples.'

## URINE

Robert Boyle (1627–91) had a fondness for preparing phosphorus from urine. Especially his own. But this was not his only talent. Born at Lismore Castle, Co. Waterford, Boyle had thirteen brothers and sisters, which may have been the reason for his removal to Eton at the age of eight. Thanks to the education he received there, he went on to show for the first time by practical experiment that Galileo was correct in stating that in a vacuum a feather and a lump of lead dropped together land simultaneously. He also showed that there was an inverse relationship between pressure and volume of air, thereafter known as 'Boyle's Law'.

A deeply religious man, Boyle learned Hebrew, Greek and Syriac in order to study the Bible, and in his will founded the Boyle Lectures, not on science but on the defence of Christianity against unbelievers. He died on the last day of 1691, though there is no suggestion that it was the result of a hernia. Perhaps this is because a fellow Lismore man, St Cathal, is the patron saint of people who sufferer from that condition.

Traditionally, the bladder of a goat, filled with human urine, dried in a chimney, then ground down to a powder and mixed with raw onion was rubbed into the head as a cure for baldness.

There is no V in the Irish alphabet

### VALENTIA
Europe's most western harbour. From this small island the first transatlantic cable was run in 1857.

### VALENTINE, SAINT
Of a number of saints of the same name, at least one is buried in Whitefriars Street Church in Dublin.

Daniel Corkery, the Cork-born artist, storyteller and critic who was a teacher of Frank O'Connor, and who is best remembered for his *The Hidden Ireland*, was born on St Valentine's Day, 1878, and died on the last day of 1964.

### VEGETABLES
The patron saint of gardeners and vegetables is St Fiacre (or Fiacra) who lived in Ireland in the 7th century. The French word for a four-wheel cab is *fiacre*, because when they first began to appear on the streets of Paris, around 1620, their stand was close by the Hôtel Saint-Fiacre. St Fiacre's feast day is variously given as 31 August and 1 September.

Fiacre is also the patron saint of those afflicted by venereal disease and haemorrhoids, as Henry V discovered when his troops ransacked the shrine of the Irish saint at Meaux in France. Henry died on 31 August 1422, if not actually on the saint's feast day, at least within 24 hours of it. The cause of death was a form of dysentry popularly known as St Fiacre's Disease.

(See **Swift, Jonathan**)

## VENOM
Although there are no native snakes in Ireland, **Shakespeare**, for one, seems to have detected traces of venom: 'Now for our Irish wars:/We must supplant those rough rug-headed kerns,/Which live like venom where no venom else/But only they, have privilege to live' – *Richard II* (II.i).

## VERNE, JULES (1828–1905)
Science fiction writer whose novel *P'tit Bonhomme*, published in 1892, is set in Ireland towards the end of the 19th century.

## VICTORIA, QUEEN (1819–1901)
Queen of the United Kingdom (1837–1901) who on a visit to Dublin bought from the Lord Mayor the Irish State Coach (built in 1852), which is to this day used for British royal occasions such as weddings and funerals. Not the most popular of English queens with some sections of the Irish press, a number of suspected deliberate misprints appeared in the papers during her visit to Dublin, the most memorable being that the Queen 'pissed' instead of 'passed' over O'Connell

Bridge. **George Bernard Shaw**, too, had been happy to make known his views on her: 'Nowadays a parlourmaid as ignorant as Queen Victoria was when she came to the throne would be classed as mentally defective.'

## VICTORIA CROSS

A military decoration awarded for bravery and named for Queen Victoria. Since the first VC was awarded to an Irishman, C. David Lucas, who threw a live shell overboard from HMS *Hecla* on 21 June 1845 while serving as a mate in the Baltic, many Irish men have received VCs. Most notable among these is Major Edward 'Mick' Mannock from Cork, who was the most noted air ace of World War I, having shot down a total of 73 enemy planes. When Mannock's VC came up for sale in 1992, it fetched a world record £132,000.

Athlone-born Thomas Flinn was only 15 years and 3 months old at the time of the action for which he won his VC (28 November 1857).

## VIKINGS

Savage, rapacious invaders from Scandinavia who came to Ireland in AD 795 and chased the monks up into their **round towers**. Many of the Vikings who were not particularly interested in rape or pillage, and were lucky enough not to be driven out by Strongbow some time later, integrated with the natives and became *Hiberniores Hibernicis ipsis*, or 'more Irish than the Irish themselves'. This is the reason why much of modern Irish marine and nautical vocabulary has a Scandinavian origin.

The Vikings also found time to run a kind of protection racket with the Irish chieftains. Failure to make returns for same resulted in the loss of a facial accessory, hence the name of this contribution, *airgead shrona* or 'nose money'.

The present Civic Offices in Dublin are built on an

important Viking site. Despite enormous popular protest by the citizens of Dublin, led by F. X. Martin (b. 1922), one of the editors of the ten-volume *New History of Ireland*, work went ahead on the buildings commonly known as 'the bunkers', after a design by the architect Sam Stephenson (b. 1933). Stephenson said: 'I want to leave my mark.'

## VIRGINS

Much has been said of Ireland and virgins. **George Bernard Shaw** was a virgin until he was 29, and when he finally did make the break he must have regretted it, because he spent the next 15 years in a mood of abstinence. However, it is that most famous of virgins, the Virgin Mary (*c.* 22 BC–*c.* AD 40), who is closest to the hearts of the Irish. The woman who is credited with at least one appearance on Irish soil, officially recognized by the Catholic church, has also appeared on the cover of *Time* magazine more than any other person or deity (ten times. Rock star **Bono** and **U2**, however, are the first Irish rock band to make the grade).

On 21 August 1879, the year poet and patriot **Patrick Pearse** was born (though his famous poem 'The Mother' is not about her), the Virgin Mary is said to have appeared in Knock, a small town in Co. Mayo, and a place that remains to this day a centre of devotional pilgrimage. Interestingly, little is known about the Mother of God. In fact, after Christ's Ascension into heaven and the visit of the Holy Spirit in his place, the authors of the Bible never mention the Virgin again and no one even bothers to say where or how she died. It is this fact, perhaps, that created the notion she finished her days in Ireland.

Another holy woman who had connections with virgins was Nano Nagle (1728–84). Born in Ballygriffin, near Mallow, Co. Cork, Nagle, the founder of the Presentation Order of nuns, was given permission by Pope Pius VI 'to erect... houses for the reception of pious virgins...'. In recent years, though this may not be directly connected, vocations to the Order have fallen dramatically.

**Oliver St John Gogarty** might not have approved of Nagle's mission. 'Virgins have done a deal of harm in this island,' he said. 'And marriage does nothing to soften their dissatisfaction with life. It cannot be all the fault of the men. It must be the hardness of our women that is driving men to politics. A little slogan formed itself in my mind, a cry to the women of Ireland: "More petting, less politics."'

A law passed in Youghal, Co. Cork, in 1610 carried fines of up to £40 for the deflowering of virgins.

There is no W in the Irish alphabet.

### WALLETS
A convicted murderer who lured wayfarers to their
deaths and then sold their corpses for between £8 and
£14 was William Burke (1792–1829), finally captured
and hanged for a murder in Edinburgh. It is said his
skin was used to make wallets.

### WARTS
Though not the most fondly remembered of men in
Irish history, **Oliver Cromwell** was nevertheless not
one to have his weaknesses concealed. In a letter to
the artist who was to paint a portrait of him,
Cromwell wrote: 'Mr Lely, I desire you would use all
your skill to paint my picture truly like me, and not
flatter me at all; but remark all these roughnesses,
pimples, warts and everything as you see me, otherwise... I never will pay a farthing for it.'

For a clearer complexion, Cromwell might have
used the wild flower Irish Spurge which is recommended to combat warts. However, it is also used by
poachers for killing fish.

## WATERWAYS, INLAND

The longest river in these islands at 214 miles is the Shannon. Along its route are a number of monastic settlements, most famous of which is Clonmacnois, and it was up the Shannon that the **Vikings** made their way as far as Lough Ree. The Shannon is connected to Dublin by two canals, built in the mid-1700s, the Grand (main line 82 miles long) and the Royal (90 miles long); the former joins it at Shannon harbour in the south while the latter joins it at Tarmonbarry near its source. The Royal Canal, built after the Grand, was begun by a disgruntled ex-employee of the Grand Canal Company in an attempt to take away their trade. In the event, the project left him bankrupt.

## WEATHER

The subject of endless comment and discussion in Ireland. Among those things to be on the watch out for as signs of bad weather to come are: cats scratching trees, listless hens, ducks quacking unusually loudly, rooks flying erratically, herons on their own, brown frogs, crying peacocks, flies annoying pigs, flies being easily caught by fish and dogs eating grass.

## WELLINGTON, DUKE OF (1769–1852)

The man who defeated Napoleon at the Battle of Waterloo was born in Merrion Street, Dublin, but he was not very proud of the fact. 'Not everything born in a stable is a horse,' he said of his place of origin. Nevertheless, despite his lack of respect, someone took on the considerable trouble of commemorating his famous victory by planting trees on the Lyons Estate in Co. Kildare in the formation of the troops as they had stood to face each other at Waterloo.

(See **Horses; Emmet, Robert; Prime Ministers**)

### WHALEY, BUCK (1766–1800)

(See **Bets**)

### WHEELS

Though the Irish do not claim to have invented the wheel, wheels have their place in Irish history.

In the village of Moneen, Co. Clare, priests went to great lengths to avoid trouble under the Penal Laws of 1695. Where priests in other parts of the country went into woods and up mountains to say mass in secret, the clergy in this village near Kilkee built a little ark on wheels which could be pushed into the sea with the priest on board so that he might say mass for the people gathered on the shore, without breaking the rule that no service should take place on land. The ark survives today in the local church.

Still on the subject of wheels and priests, the first priest to be ordained in a wheelchair was Fr Leo Close (1934–77) in 1959, and it was he who founded the Irish Wheelchair Association.

In January 1994, the *Irish Independent* reported an unusual attack on an elderly couple in Dublin. Three men forced their way into the home of William Cruise (84), and his wife May (85), and stole £168. Thinking quickly, however, Mrs Cruise locked the door of the bedroom in which she and her husband had been bundled by the raiders, and managed to climb out a window to raise the alarm. Police described as 'bizarre' the fact that the gang leader was confined to a wheelchair.

### WHISKEY

The Irish version is spelled with an 'e'. Otherwise known as *uisce beatha,* the 'water of life'. By law, Irish whiskey must be allowed to mature for at least five years prior to being sold.

Membership of the infamous Hellfire Club in Dublin was restricted to those who could down ten glasses of whiskey before dinner followed by a quart afterwards. One of the founders of the Club was Colonel John St Leger who died in 1799 and who founded the horse race which is called after him. He also became the Governor of Ceylon, better known for tea than whiskey.

(See **Carolan, Turlough**)

## WHITE HOUSE, THE
America's Presidential residence was designed by James Hoban (1762–1831) who came from Callan, Co. Kilkenny, and who, on 14 July 1981, was the first person ever to be honoured on a joint Irish-US postage stamp.

## WHOOPING COUGH
One cure for whooping cough is to boil a mouse in milk and then to drink it. Another is to pass the afflicted patient backwards and forwards over and under the body of a donkey.

## WILDE, OSCAR (1854–1900)
Editor of *Woman's World* from 1887 to 1889. The author of plays, prose and poems, Wilde fell from fame to infamy in London after a legal action taken by the Marquess of Queensberry that left him branded as a sodomite. (Oscar had been dating the Marquess's son, though he was not above marrying Constance Lloyd in May 1884.) Some of Wilde's best works, 'The Ballad of Reading Gaol' and *De Profundis*, were written during his subsequent two-year stretch in prison. He died in Paris in 1900, converting to Catholicism on the day of his death. His last words were reported as: 'That wallpaper is killing me. One of us must go.'

He is buried in the cemetery of Père Lachaise in Paris. The statue above his grave was unveiled in 1914 by poet and magician Aleister Crowley, one of the few people of note who dared be associated with the flamboyant Wilde even after his death.

(See **Swift, Jonathan**; **Bollix**; **Robinson, Mary**)

## WILDE, SIR WILLIAM (1815–76)

Oscar's da. A celebrated eye and ear specialist, Sir William was born in Moytura house near Cong, Co. Mayo. Cong is thought to have been the site of the legendary First Battle of Moytura, one of the earliest mentioned in Irish legend. The Second Battle of Moytura actually took place in Co. Sligo and saw the defeat of the Formorians by Lugh Lámhfhada and the **Tuatha Dé Danann**.

## WIND

Thomas Romney Robinson (1792–1882), the Dublin-born director of Armagh Observatory, was the man responsible for the invention of the Cup-Anemometer in 1846, a device for measuring the speed of wind. The largest windmill in these islands, and one of only three operational in Ireland, is Blennerville Windmill, near Tralee in Co. Kerry.

The Beaufort Scale, which is used to measure the force of the wind, was devised by Dublin-born Admiral Sir Francis Beaufort.

(See **Flatulence**)

## WINDSCALE

Real name of Sellafield Nuclear Plant in Cumbria, England. Despite concern from the citizens and government of Ireland about suspected leaks there, the plant continues to operate. However, after the world's second-largest ever radioactive leak on 10 October 1957, British Nuclear Fuels finally took radical and decisive action. They changed the name.

## WITCHES

The last witch-burning in Ireland took place at Cloneen, Co. Tipperary, as late as 1895 (the same year as **Oscar Wilde**'s famous court appearance before Carson). However it hardly qualifies as an official execution. The burning followed an argument between two elderly women during which one became convinced of the other's supernatural nature. 'I have the old witch killed,' said the woman after the deed. 'I got power from the Blessed Virgin to kill her. She came to me at 3 o'clock yesterday and told me to kill her or I would be plagued with rats and mice.'

The enthusiasm of the Catholic and Protestant churches for putting women to the test of fire came from their literal interpretation of the biblical line, 'Thou shalt not suffer a witch to live' (Exodus 22:18).

Accused witches should presumably have prayed to St Dymphna who, among other things, is the patron saint of those possessed by the devil, which seems a bit pointless since those so possessed are unlikely to pray to Christian saints.

Witches in the guise of hares are said to attempt to milk cows on May mornings. Hares, especially in May, must therefore be shot on sight if seen near a herd. Witches were more likely, however, to appear as cats, as was the habit of the famous 14th-century Kilkenny witch, Dame Alice Kytler.

### WITTGENSTEIN, LUDWIG (1889–1951)
Austrian-born philosopher who lived for a time in Ireland where he wrote the second volume of his *Philosophical Investigations* between 1947 and 1949. His native Austria is only 225 square miles smaller than Ireland.

Charlie Chaplin, whose *The Great Dictator* was a thinly disguised satire of the Austrian-born leader of the Third Reich, Adolf Hitler, was, like Wittgenstein, born in 1889. His mother was Hannah Hill, who came from Cork.

### WOBBLIES
(See **Connolly, James**)

## WOLVES
Wolves were still so plentiful in Ireland, even after the stripping of much of the great forests, that a public hunt had to be held in Castleknock, Dublin, in December 1652. A bitch's head was worth the considerable sum of £6.

The last wolf in Ireland was reputedly killed in Carlow in 1786.

## WOODBINE
Wild honeysuckle.

Also a brand of filterless cigarette.

Woodbine Willie was the nickname of Jesuit Father Willy Doyle, who was born in Dalkey, Co. Dublin, in 1873. As a chaplain during World War I, Doyle was said to have doled out the cigarettes to soldiers in the trenches, earning him the sobriquet. The above small kindness seems enormous in comparison to the hardships he meanwhile inflicted on himself, as evidenced by his private diaries which recount his self-mortifications in the name of Christ. In these Doyle was nothing if not imaginative. One entry reads: 'I tried with a penknife to cut the sweet name of Jesus on my breast. It was not a success, for I suppose my courage failed; I did try a heated iron, but it caused an ugly sore.' Undeterred by the amount of senseless cruelty already existing in the world, he went on to wade naked through beds of nettles, to stand, again naked, in freezing water until almost passing out, and then to follow this with 'what I can only call a flogging from head to toe with red hot needles'. Once thought to be a candidate for canonization, Doyle is now, unsurprisingly, a cause of some embarrassment to his order.

There is no X in the Irish alphabet.

**XANTHODONT** (zan'thó-dont)
A person with yellowed teeth. The word could be used to describe **Eamon de Valera** after his self-confessed boyhood habit of smoking turf.

There is no Y in the Irish alphabet.

## YAHOO

The 'satirical' magazine, *Punch*, one of the longest-running journals in these islands, finally ceased publication in 1992. 130 years earlier, however, it could still get away with the following: 'A gulf, certainly, does appear to yawn between the Gorilla and the Negro. The woods and wilds of Africa do not exhibit an example of any intermediate animal. But... a creature manifestly between the gorilla and the negro is to be met with in some of the lowest districts of London and Liverpool... It comes from Ireland, whence it has contrived to migrate; it belongs, in fact, to a tribe of Irish savages; the lowest species of the Irish Yahoo. When conversing with its kind it talks a sort of gibberish. It is, moreover, a climbing animal, and may sometimes be seen ascending a ladder laden with a hod of bricks... The somewhat superior ability of the Irish Yahoo to utter articulate sounds may suffice to prove that it is a development and not, as some imagine, a degeneration of the gorilla.'

**YEATS, JACK BUTLER (1871–1957)**
London-born Impressionist painter brother of William.

**YEATS, WILLIAM BUTLER (1865–1939)**
Born in Sandymount, Dublin. Poet, senator, co-founder of the Abbey Theatre and mystic, Yeats attended his first seance in 1886: 'I sat motionless for a while and then my whole body moved like a suddenly unrolled watch-spring and I was thrown backward on the wall.' Yeats, who refused a knighthood in 1915, proposed marriage to three different women in the year 1917 alone (after proposing to **Maud Gonne**, he was later to try his luck with her daughter, Iseult). When awarded the Nobel Prize for Literature in 1923, Yeats celebrated by cooking sausages.

(See **Coins**)

**YES**
English word for which there is no exact Irish equivalent. This explains what, for the visitor, appears an annoying and peculiarly Irish habit, that of returning a roundabout answer to a simple question. E.g. 'Was that you I saw yesterday on the way to work with a shovel over your shoulder and a cigarette in your mouth?' Answer: 'It was me you saw yesterday on the way to work with a shovel over my shoulder and a cigarette in my mouth.'

(See **No**)

**YETI**
It was on the 104th anniversary of the birth of **Bram Stoker**, creator of *Dracula*, that the first photographs of footprints claimed to belong to the abominable snowman were taken on the lower slopes of Mount Everest.

There is no Z in the Irish alphabet.

### ZENDA, THE PRISONER OF
Film made by Rex Ingram (1893–1950) who was born in Rathmines, Dublin, and studied Law at Trinity College before moving to Yale and eventually to Hollywood where he converted to Islam. Another Irishman who got into the movies, and became a producer in Hollywood and England, was IRA soldier of the War of Independence Emmet Dalton.

### ZORBA THE GREEK
Anthony Quinn, the star of the famous film, was born in Mexico on 21 April 1915 to an Irish father, Frank Quinn.

### ZOZIMUS
The name by which the Dublin street poet and balladeer Michael Moran (1749–1846) was better known. His 'In Praise of Potheen' gives some indication of his style: 'O, long life to the man who invinted potheen/Sure the Pope ought to make him a martyr/If myself was this moment Victoria, our Queen/I'd drink nothing but whiskey and wather.'